Bob's Book of Dog Names

JAMES CARRON

Amenta Publishing

www.amenta.ink

Bob's Book of Dog Names

For Bob

Bob's Book of Dog Names

Edition 1 - 2021/22

By James Carron

First published 2021 by Amenta Publishing

Copyright © James Carron 2021

ISBN 9798518382770

The right of James Carron to be identified as the author of this work has been asserted by him in accordance with the Copyright, Designs and Patents Act 1988.

All rights reserved. No part of this publication may be reproduced, stored in a retrieval system, or transmitted in any form, or by any means, electronic, mechanical, photocopying, recording or otherwise, without permission in writing from the publisher.

Contents

Introduction	4

Part 1

Most Popular

Top 100 – Female	9
Top 100 – Male	11
Top by Breed	13
Big Dogs	14
Small Dogs	14

Trends

Food	16
Alcoholic Drinks	17
Celebrities	18
Pop Stars	23

Colours

White	24
Black	25
Brown	26
Yellow/Gold	26
Red	27
Grey/Blue/Silver	28

Themes

Movies	29
Disney	32
Cartoons	35
Soap Stars	37
Blue Peter	38
Sitcoms & Series	39
Literature	40
Video Games	40
Harry Potter	41
Outlander	42
Games of Thrones	42
The Gods	44
Stars & Constellations	46
Royal Dogs	47
Heroic Dogs	49
Working Dogs	52
Nobility	53
World Leaders	54
Explorers	55
Scientists	55
Great Outdoors	56
Trees & Fauna	59
Seas & Oceans	59
Technology	60
Cars	61
Perfect Pairs	62
Terrific Trios	66

Part 2

A-Z	67

Bob's Book of Dog Names

Introduction

As parent to a new dog, whether it be a puppy or an older mixed breed adopted from a rescue shelter, one of the most important aspects of welcoming your pet into your family and home is choosing a name.

Some people are lucky – they have the perfect moniker in mind. But you are not quite so sure, which is why you bought this book. So, where to start?

 Have fun

Importantly, the process should be fun. But, as you have probably discovered, it is not necessarily easy. Finding the perfect name for your pooch can be difficult. It is, after all, a long-term commitment and something the whole family should agree on. And, as we all know, garnering agreement among everyone in a household can be a long, drawn-out process peppered with arguments and debate along the way.

 Some science

You may wish to look to the science and psychology of dog naming. There are a few key recommendations that pet professionals tend to agree on.

The most consistent piece of advice is to select a short name with just one or two syllables. This will quickly attract your dog's attention.

Animal behaviourists say dogs respond well to short and choppy noises while longer, softer and more drawn-out sounds are less likely to make them sit up and take notice.

Some experts advise picking a name that ends in a short *a* sound or a long vowel while others recommend names ending in *y* because of the gentle, easy-to-pronounce sound. The most popular dogs' names – **Bella**, **Luna** and **Poppy** for girls and **Milo**, **Teddy** and **Buddy** for boys – illustrate this well.

To help your dog distinguish its name from ambient noise, chit chat and other background distractions, you could choose something with a strident consonant or blend, such as an *s* or *sh*, or a crisp, commanding consonant like a *k* or hard *c*.

Names with a generous sprinkling of vowels attract a dog's attention too as they pick up on the changing frequency in the tone at a much higher level than we humans do.

It is a good idea to avoid names that sound like or rhyme with cue words and commands you are likely to use in training. Anything similar to *sit, stay, heel, come, fetch* or *no* could be easily confused by your pet. **Kit**, for example, sounds like *sit*, **Fletch** like *fetch*, and **Beau** like *no*.

Don't worry if you choose to ignore this – **Beau** ranks in the top ten of dog names in the UK, indicating that countless others do too.

Steer away from common, everyday words that are used frequently in conversations, otherwise your dog will be constantly looking up at you while you chat way on the phone.

Selecting a name that is too similar to those of other pets in the household, or family members, will lead to confusion and, if you plan to name your puppy after a member of the family, make sure it's OK with them first.

 Keep it clean

While much of the scientific advice can be happily ignored, it is important to avoid names that others may find offensive or embarrassing or which include swear words, racist or insulting language or crass slang terms, or which have negative undertones.

The German fascist dictator Adolf Hitler had a loyal canine called **Blondi**, which is a great name for a dog and which few would associate with him. But call your pup Adolf or indeed Hitler and you will not be popular down the local park.

Similarly, others may take offence to a name like Chucky, or Cujo, the rabid St Bernard in Stephen King's eponymous horror.

Remember too that the name you select will be used in places like the vet, on pet insurance paperwork or might need to be quoted or plastered over a poster if your pet goes missing.

Science and psychology play their part, but at the end of the day it really is down to you and your family what you pick, and most people just plump for a name they like.

When friends, colleagues and relatives discover you are getting a new dog, chances are they will swamp you with suggestions. Problem is, you might not like any of their ideas. Don't be swayed, bullied or browbeaten into accepting any of them, unless, of course, someone comes up with something you like.

If you are still struggling to find a simple, meaningful moniker that is easy to pronounce and reflects your dog's looks or personality, inspiration is everywhere.

 Make it meaningful

We all have a favourite book, box set, movie or cartoon character, whether contemporary or from our childhood, a personality, real or fictitious, human, animal or alien, that evokes happiness, positive feelings, fond memories or just a tinge of nostalgia. Maybe there's scope for a name there?

Dogs are naturally intuitive creatures and will recognise these warm and positive feelings.

Perhaps you have a favourite sportsman or woman or team, or maybe a favourite film or TV actor or character, pop star or musician. Many people like to name their dogs after well-known celebrities, politicians or historical figures. **Bojo** and **Boris** became popular when Boris Johnson became Prime Minister in 2019 while, across the pond, a growing number of dogs were christened **Donald** after Donald Trump took office in the White House in 2017.

If you love the great outdoors (and your dog will undoubtedly share that passion), place names and plants like **Devon**, **Isla**, **Scotia**, **Skye**, **Windsor**, **Bracken**, **Heather**, **Ivy** and **Holly** are always popular.

 **Trends**

Increasingly fashionable are names based on favourite foods or drinks. **Twiglet**, **Hobnob**, **Cupcake**, **Oreo**, **Mocha**, **Gin**, **Guinness** and **Prosecco** are all on trend right now. But this is nothing new. The Queen named two of her Corgis **Whisky** and **Sherry** back in 1955 and owned cocker spaniels called **Bisto** and **Oxo**.

If you are welcoming a pair of dogs to the family, you might want to consider christening them after a well-known double act, such as **Ant** and **Dec**, **Tom** and **Jerry** or **Holmes** and **Watson**, or things that traditionally come in twos, like **Salt** and **Pepper**, **Mac** and **Cheese** and **Coffee** and **Doughnuts**.

Dodge pairing two names that sound very similar and bear in mind that inevitably there will come a time when you are calling out only one of the names.

Trends are useful for those seeking a popular name but beware of following them too closely. Celebrities come and go, some quicker than others, and we can be fickle with our favourites.

You might name your puppy after one of the Kardashians or a character from *Games of Thrones* now and, in five years, sit down and wonder *'why did I do that?'*, while events like the global pandemic of 2020/21, which spawned names like **Covie**, **Rona** and **Corona**, may soon go out of fashion.

You and your dog will be carrying the name around for (hopefully) at least a decade so it needs to be something enduring that you can both live with long-term.

There will always be a place for traditional, long established names like **Rover** and **Fido**, but there is no harm in pushing the boundaries and coming up with something truly unique, a name that resonates with you, whatever your inspiration.

Make it a name you love and one your pup responds well to.

 **Try it out**

It is a good idea to select a few potential options to start and, once you have your shortlist, try them out individually.

Repeatedly say the name out loud, perhaps stand on your back doorstep and call it out across the garden, just to see how it sounds. You must be willing to both say it and shout it, often in public, repeatedly.

Does the name roll off the tongue easily? Does it sound and feel natural? Are you comfortable with it, or is it embarrassing? If you wince when you say it out loud, it is probably not one to pursue.

If the name is longer and one that might spawn nicknames, try them out too. **Chipper**, for example, could breed **Chip**, **Chips**, **Chippy** or **Mister Chips**.

If you already have your new dog, try out the name for a few days and see how he responds. There is no harm in changing early on, before your dog has had a chance to become accustomed to its potential moniker.

 Stick with it

Once you have chosen a name, stick with it. If you are unsure, your dog will be too. There is no harm in making a couple of changes, but the quicker you commit, the quicker your pup will respond positively when he hears his name.

If you and your family are happy with a name, that is really all that matters. Your dog may answer to it, but despite being the centre of attention, he or she really has no knowledge of its source, inspiration or popularity.

If you adopt a rescue dog and are not keen on keeping the name it comes with, experts say it is OK to change. Often stray and rescue dogs are renamed in kennels anyway as little of their history is known so chances are they will not have had a chance to get used to what their carers call them. You may want to go with something that has a similar sound or the same number of syllables, but that is not vital. The important thing is that you spend lots of time teaching your dog his new name and associating it with positive experiences, such as praise or treats.

 Say my name

With your dog now named, always quote it in a bright, cheery voice and if your dog responds by bounding over to you or looking up at you, give him plenty of praise, pats, strokes and cuddles, and a treat. In this way, your pet learns that whenever he hears his name, good things happen. If a dog knows there's praise or a treat to be had, he will always respond.

There are many positive ways of teaching your dog its new name. Repeat the name just before you put the lead on, make a fuss of him, feed him, invite him to play a game, or do anything else that he finds fun or enjoyable.

Get everyone in the household involved. Encourage family members to occasionally call his new name and reward him with praise and treats. Keep the momentum up and practice in different rooms of the house, outside in the garden and when out on walks. This will continue throughout training and the rest of your dog's life.

Now, let's find that perfect name…

Good luck!

Paws a moment in your quest to find the perfect name to read the snippets of information scattered through the book…

Listings

This book is split into two parts:

 Part 1

The first part begins by ranking the 100 most popular names of 2020/21 before exploring trends and offering ideas for names based on the breed, size and colour of your pup.

Thereafter names are grouped into themes, the pages to read if you want to name your dog after an heroic hound from history, a famous explorer or a classic car. Here you can check out movie star dogs, cartoon canines and celebrity pups or, if you fancy something with a bit more pedigree, Royal rovers.

 Part 2

The second part is an A-Z listing containing over 3000 names.

Most Popular

Every year, pet insurers, animal charities and dog businesses compile and publish lists of the most popular dogs' names.

In addition to highlighting the nation's favourites, they also reveal growing trends among dog owners, and names that are falling out of fashion.

The following Top 100s are based on data published *by Compare the Market, More Than, Rover* and *Blue Cross.*

Top 100 – Female Dogs

 1-10

Bella

Poppy

Lolo

Luna

Bailey

Ruby

Daisy

Molly

Coco

Rosie

 11-25

Millie

Willow

Roxy

Tilly

Bonnie

Nala

Marley

Skye

Holly

Belle

Lily

Loki

Lexi

Winnie

Honey

 26-50

Lucy

Maggie

Maisie

Dolly

Lottie

Mabel

Betty

Pippa

Penny

Minnie

Jess

Bob's Book of Dog Names

Mia	Indie
Sam	Nova
Amber	Piper
Jessie	Ivy
Ellie	Layla
Beau	Dixie
Lady	Samantha
Milly	Peanut
Olive	Sophie
Phoebe	Sadie
Cookie	Flo
Pip	
Peggy	🐾 **76-100**
Pixie	Juno
🐾 **51-75**	Boo
	Brandy
Stella	Summer
Sasha	Elsa
Meg	Harley
Mollie	Sally
Cassie	Ginger
Maya	Maddie
Sky	Storm
Tessa	Dottie
Gracie	Marley
Tia	Heidi
Frankie	Darcey
Madison	Kiki
Cleo	Ariel
Zoe	Leia

Princess
Pepper
Callie
Maisy
Sandy
Abby
Suki
Jasmine

Top 100 – Male Dogs

1-10

Alfie
Milo
Max
Charlie
Buddy
Teddy
Oscar
Bob
Hugo
Archie

11-25

Reggie
Dexter
Barney
Bear
Monty
Toby

Frank
Cooper
Buster
George
Ralph
Frankie
Bertie
Bruno
Harley

26-50

Ollie
Bruce
Blue
Rocky
Winston
Murphy
Jasper
Freddie
Jack
Stanley
Rocco
Chester
Henry
Bobby
Billy
Harvey
Sam
Ziggy
Simba

Bob's Book of Dog Names

Rolo	Diesel
Woody	Finn
Rufus	Dave
Tyson	
Louis	**76-100**
Ozzy	Theo
	Enzo
51-75	Arlo
Rex	Paddy
Wilson	Hector
Ernie	Ben
Riley	Jake
Beau	Louie
Coco	Cody
Lucky	Benny
Rusty	Basil
Duke	Fudge
Otis	Brodie
Eddie	Oliver
Hunter	Bentley
Shadow	Boris
Patch	Benji
Pablo	Mylo
Casper	Angus
Rupert	Tommy
Dylan	Mac
Zeus	Thor
Gizmo	Gus
Ronnie	Luke
Baxter	Sparky

Most Popular by Breed

Airedale Terrier – Monty
Akita – Luna
Alaskan Malamute – Luna
American Bulldog – Luna
Bassett Hound – Bertie
Beagle – Bella
Bernese Mountain Dog – Bob
Bichon Frise – Teddy
Border Collie – Max
Border Terrier – Archie
Boston Terrier – Luna
Boxer – Bella
Bulldog – Winston
Bullmastiff – Bob
Cairn Terrier – Archie
Cavalier King Charles Spaniel – Charlie
Chihuahua – Coco
Chow Chow – Bear
Cockapoo – Teddy
Cocker Spaniel – Poppy
Dachshund – Frank
Dalmatian – Daisy
Doberman – Luna

English Bulldog – Winston
English Mastiff – Bob
English Springer Spaniel – Bella
Farm Collie – Meg
Flat Coater Retriever – Monty
Fox Terrier – Ted
French Bulldog – Hugo
French Mastiff – Hooch
German Shepherd – Max
German Longhaired Pointer – Horace
German Shorthaired Pointer – Bob
Golden Retriever – Bailey
Great Dane – Bob
Greyhound – Bob
Jack Russell Terrier – Jack
Husky – Loki
Irish Setter – Ruby
Irish Wolfhound – Bob
Labradoodle – Teddy
Labrador – Bella
Labrador Retriever – Max
Leonberger – Bob
Lhasa Apso – Alfie
Lurcher – Poppy
Maltese – Teddy
Miniature Poodle – Teddy
Miniature Schnauzer – Alfie
Newfoundland – Bear
Old English Bulldog – Luna

Bob's Book of Dog Names

Old English Sheepdog – Bob
Patterdale Terrier – Max
Pomeranian – Teddy
Pug – Bella
Pyrenean Mountain Dog – Bear
Rhodesian Ridgeback – Ruby
Rottweiler – Roxy
Rough Collie – Laddie
St Bernard – Bob
Scottish Terrier – Angus
Shar Pei – Bella
Shih Tzu – Teddy
Siberian Husky – Luna
Staffordshire Bull Terrier – Bella
Standard Poodle – Lola
Toy Poodle – Teddy
Weimaraner – Luna
West Highland White Terrier – Alfie
Whippet – Luna
West Highland Terrier – Bob
Yorkshire Terrier – Poppy

The Tibetan Mastiff is the strongest dog breed in the world due to its gentle nature around the house but aggressive behaviour towards strangers.

Inspired by...

Big Dogs

Size is not everything, but some names just suit bigger dogs better...

Bear
Beethoven
Bernard
Bertha
Boss
Bruiser
Bruno
Brutus
Burly
Butch
Cassius
Chief
Colossus
Conan
Goliath
Grizzle
Jumbo
Hercules
Hulk
Hunter
King
Kong
Max
Maximus
Mega

Moose
Orca
Rambo
Rip
Rocky
Spartan
Sultan
Thor
Thunder
Titan
Tyson
Wolf
Zeus

Foo-Foo
Hobbit
Micro
Milo
Minnie
Moppet
Munchkin
Nipper
Peanut
Pebble
Petal
Pip
Pixie
Shrimp
Snowdrop
Thimble
Tinkerbell
Tiny
Toto
Trixie
Widget
Wookiee

Inspired by...

Small Dogs

And some suit petite pooches.
Baby
Bambi
Bea
Bean
Berry
Bitty
Bluebell
Button
Coco
Cookie
Cupcake
Elf

The Border Collie is considered to be the dog with the highest IQ, followed by the Poodle, German Shepherd and Golden Retriever.

Bob's Book of Dog Names

Trends

Like baby names, the popularity of dog names is heavily influenced by fluctuating trends that reflect, at any given time, our likes and interests, the events going on around us and the people who influence us, whether they be politicians, pop stars or TV characters. The popularity of **Bella**, for example, appears to be linked to both the *Twilight* TV series and books and the *Harry Potter* movies and books.

In 2020, the global pandemic saw Covid-19 based names appear, but more popular was a trend towards food and alcohol with **Brandy**, **Cookie** and **Peanut** rising through the Top 100, and newcomers like **Twiglet** and **Hobnob** gaining ground.

Inspired by...

Food

Aero

Barley

Basil

Bean

Berry

Biscotti

Biscuit

Bounty

Brioche

Brownie

Burrito

Butterscotch

Caramel

Cocoa

Chip

Chomp

Churro

Chutney

Cinnamon

Clove

Cookie

Cupcake

Daim

Dijon

Doughnut/Donut

Dorito

Fig

Flapjack

Fudge

Ginger

Hobnob

Honey

Kale

Maple

Muffin

Mustard
Nacho
Noodle
Nugget
Nutella
Peaches
Peanut
Pesto
Pickles
Pistachio
Plum
Pretzel
Pringles
Pudding
Ripple
Rogan
Rosemary
Rye
Skittles
Sugar
Taco
Tikka
Toast
Toffee
Twiglet
Twix
Wafer
Waffles
Wasabi
Wispa

Inspired by...

Alcoholic Drinks

Bourbon
Brandy
Cava
Champagne
Chardonnay
Cider
Foster
Gin
Guinness
Macallan
Margarita
Martini
Mateus
Merlot
Miller
Mojito
Pinot
Prosecco
Rosé
Rum
Sake
Sambuca
Scotch
Sherry
Tequila
Whisky/Whiskey

Bob's Book of Dog Names

Inspired by...

Hot Drinks

Americano

Assam

Barista

Brew

Cappuccino

Chai

Cherry

Coffee

Cortado

Cubano

Earl Grey

Espresso

Jasmine

Java

Lady Grey

Latte

Matcha

Mocha

Rooibos

Bred as a hunting dog, its soft mouth ideal for picking up downed game birds, the Golden Retriever originated in Scotland in the mid-19th century. Its good nature meant it quickly became popular as a pet.

Inspired by...

Celebrities

The names celebrities christened their dogs (and, perhaps surprisingly, most of them are fairly sensible). There is a growing trend for rescue dogs among celebrity owners.

Ace – *Rat Terrier*, Carrie Underwood

Alfred – *Labradoodle*, Matthew Perry

Allegra – *Poodle/Terrier mix*, Hugh Jackman

Angus – *Border Terrier*, Lorraine Kelly

Asia – *French Bulldog*, Lady Gaga,

Atticus – *German Shepherd*, Jake Gyllenhaal

Bambi – *Chihuahua,* Paris Hilton

Batman – *Yorkipoo*, Demi Lovato

Baxter – *Labrador mix*, Ryan Reynolds

Baylor – *Siberian Husky mix*, Selena Gomez

Bean - *Chihuahua mix*, Miley Cyrus

Bebe – *Mixed breed*, Sandra Bullock

Berkley – *Terrier mix*, Charlize Theron

Bert – *Border Terrier*, David Walliams

18

Bertha – *Labrador*, Caitlyn Jenner

Bess – *Mixed breed*, Sienna Miller

Betty – *Chocolate Labrador*, Harrison Ford

Billie – *Mixed breed*, Ryan Reynolds

Birdie – *Golden Retriever*, Jennifer Garner

Blanco – *Mixed breed*, Brad Pitt

Blondie – *Labradoodle*, Rod Stewart and Penny Lancaster

Boo – *Yorkshire Terrier*, Johnny Depp

Boo Radley – *Puggle*, Jake Gyllenhaal

Brennan – *Boxer*, Justin Timberlake

Brutus – *Bulldog*, Dwayne 'The Rock' Johnson

Buckley – *Boxer*, Justin Timberlake

Bugs – *Border Collie/Springer Spaniel mix*, Tiger Woods

Cappy (Cappuccino Houston) – *Pit Bull*, Selma Blair

Carlos – *Chihuahua*, Matt Damon

Charlie – *King Charles Cavalier Spaniel*, Hugh Heffner

Cherry – *Mixed breed*, Arnold Schwarzenegger

Chip – *Yorkshire Terrier*, Serena Williams

Cinderella – *Yorkipoo*, Demi Lovato

Clyde – *Schnauzer mix*, Jennifer Aniston

Cha Cha – *Jack Russell Terrier*, Mariah Carey

Cody – *Australian Shepherd*, Kate Hudson

Daisy – *Maltese/Toy Poodle cross*, Jessica Simpson

Dali – *French Bulldog*, Hugh Jackman

Dama – *Maltese*, Alec Baldwin

Dexter – *Staffordshire Bull Terrier*, Dua Lipa

Diamond Baby – *Pomeranian*, Paris Hilton

Diddly – *Yorkshire Terrier*, Simon Cowell

Dodger – *Boxer mix*, Chris Evans

Dolly – *German Shepherd*, Jennifer Aniston

Dora – *Labradoodle*, Liam Hemsworth

Douglas – *Mixed breed*, Drew Barrymore

Dubois – *Bernese Mountain Dog*, Hilary Duff

Dutch – *Mixed breed*, Arnold Schwarzenegger

Einstein – *Cocker Spaniel*, George Clooney

Elvis – *French Bulldog*, Pink, and *Maltese*, Lucy Hale

Emu – *Shetland Sheepdog*, Miley Cyrus

Ernie – *Border Terrier*, David Walliams

Bob's Book of Dog Names

Esmerelda – *Chocolate Labrador*, Anne Hathaway

Esther – *Yorkshire Terrier*, Justin Bieber

Fawkes – *Shiba Inu*, Ariana Grande

Fig – *Cocker Spaniel*, David Beckham

Finn – *Australian Shepherd mix*, Amanda Seyfried

Flossie – *Chow Chow/Labrador cross*, Drew Barrymore

Forrest – *Chihuahua cross*, Leona Lewis

Foxy – *Australian Cattle Dog*, Matthew McConaughey

Freddie – *German Shepherd*, Heidi Klum

George – *Great Dane*, Jim Carey

Gertie – *Chihuahua*, Katherine Heigl

Gina – *Poodle*, Jason Biggs

Gitana – *Maltese*, Alec Baldwin

Gracie Lou – *Chihuahua*, Katherine Heigl

Hank – *Chocolate Labrador*, Reese Witherspoon

Happy – *Rottweiler/Beagle cross*, Miley Cyrus

Harold – *Havanese*, Venus Williams

Henry – *Mixed breed*, Debra Messing

Hobbs – *Bulldog*, Dwayne 'The Rock' Johnson

Hutch – *German Shepherd*, Ben Affleck

Iggy – *Mixed breed*, Josh Hartnett

Indo – *Rottweiler mix* – Will Smith

Jackie Lambchops – *Jack Russell Terrier*, Mariah Carey

JJ – *Jack Russell Terrier*, Mariah Carey

Johnny – *Mixed breed*, Charlize Theron

Julian – *Toy Poodle*, Nicole Kidman

Juno – *French Bulldog*, Michael Phelps

Karoo – *Jack Russell/Corgi mix*, Hilary Swank

Kelpie – *Mixed breed*, Harrison Ford

Ken – *Golden Retriever*, Emma Stone

Kenobi – *Terrier mix*, Anne Hathaway

Kevin – *Italian Greyhound*, Kylie Jenner

Lauren – *Springer Spaniel*, Oprah Winfrey

Layla – *Golden Retriever*, Oprah Winfrey

Legend – *French Bulldog*, Michael Phelps

Lola – *Chihuahua*, Hilary Duff, and *Australian Shepherd*, Tiger Woods

Lolita – *Pug*, Gerard Butler

Lord Chesterfield – *Great Pyrenees*, Jennifer Aniston

Louie – *Cocker Spaniel*, George Clooney

Lucky – *Chihuahua,* Britney Spears

Luke – *Golden Retriever*, Oprah Winfrey

Luna – *Husky*, Louis Smith

Maca – *Pit Bull*, Zac Efron

Major – *Black Labrador*, Reese Witherspoon

Martha Stewart – *Labrador*, Ben Affleck

Mate – *German Shepherd*, Miley Cyrus

Maverick – *Border Collie/Australian Shepherd cross*, Nina Dobrev

Matzoball – *Bulldog*, Adam Sandler

Max – *German Shepherd*, Heidi Klum

Meatball – *Bulldog*, Adam Sandler

Milie – *Basset Hound*, George Clooney

Mr Famous – *Yorkie*, Audrey Hepburn

Mrs Potts – *Labrador*, Rod Stewart and Penny Lancaster

Mrs Wallis Browning – *Standard Poodle*, Ellen Degeneres

Mocha – *French Bulldog*, Hugh Jackman

Momo – *Black Labrador*, Hilary Diff

Mona – *Boxer*, Jennifer Love Hewitt

Munchie – *Shih Tzu*, Beyonce

Muppet – *Terrier mix*, Kristen Bell

Mutley P Gore – *Jack Russell Terrier*, Mariah Carey

Myron – *Pit Bull mix*, Ariana Grande

Nash – *German Shepherd*, Reese Witherspoon

Norman – *Corgi*, Jennifer Aniston, and *Pit Bull*, Kaley Cuoco

Noodles – *Pomeranian*, Kelly Osborne

Nugget – *Teacup Poodle*, Katy Perry

Olive – *Cocker Spaniel*, David Beckham

Oliver – *Maltese/Poodle mix*, Rihanna

Pepper – *French Bulldog*, Reese Witherspoon

Pignoli – *Chihuahua*, Ariana Grande

Pipitty Jackson – *Jack Russell Terrier*, Mariah Carey

Pippa – *French Bulldog*, Chrissy Teigen

Pistol – *Yorkshire Terrier*, Johnny Depp

Polly – *Pomeranian*, Kelly Osbourne

Poppy – *Chihuahua,* Sandra Bullock

Bob's Book of Dog Names

Rocky – *Dachshund*, Declan Donnelly

Roscoe – *Doberman Pinscher*, Kevin Hart

Roxy – *Doberman Pinscher*, Kevin Hart

Ruby – *Pit Bull*, Kaley Cuoco, and *Chihuahua*, Sandra Bullock

Rumi – *Golden Retriever mix*, Hilary Swank

Sadie – *Cocker Spaniel*, Oprah Winfrey

Sage – *Cocker Spaniel*, David Beckham

Sake – *Pomeranian*, Kim Kardashian

Sammy – *Papillon*, Justin Bieber

Scarlett – *French Bulldog*, David and Victoria Beckham

Shadow – *Toy Poodle*, Vanessa Hudgens

Sheriff – *Miniature Pinscher*, Christina Ricci

Shirley – *Pit Bull*, Kaley Cuoco

Sid – *Pug*, Jessica Alba

Sidi – *Saluki mix*, Orlando Bloom

Simba – *Pomeranian*, Heidi Klum

Soba – *Pomeranian*, Kim Kardashian

Sophie – *Maltese/Toy Poodle mix*, Miley Cyrus, and *German Shepherd*, Jennifer Aniston

Spinee – *Labrador Retriever*, Denzel Washington

Squiddly – *Yorkshire Terrier*, Simon Cowell

Storm – *Black Labrador*, Ben Fogle

Strauss – *Yorkshire Terrier*, Ariana Grande

Sunday – *Mixed breed*, Natalie Portman

Sunny – *Springer Spaniel*, Oprah Winfrey

Sushi – *Pomeranian*, Kim Kardashian

Taco – *Mixed breed*, Harrison Ford

Tani – *Pit Bull*, Liam Hemsworth

Tessa – *Staffordshire Bull Terrier*, Tom Holland

Tina – *Pit Bull*, Jessica Biel

Tinkerbell – *Chihuahua*, Paris Hilton

Toulouse – *Beagle/Chihuahua mix*, Ariana Grande

Tucker – *Mixed breed*, Charlize Theron

Vida – *Mixed breed*, Demi Moore

Walter – *Shih Tzu*, Kate Hudson

Weegee – *Poodle/Schnauzer mix*, Hugh Dancy and Claire Danes

Wesley – *Chihuahua/Dachshund mix*, Kylie Jenner

Wink – *Jack Russell mix*, Selma Blair

Woody – *Standard Poodle*, Jeff Goldblum

Inspired by

🐾 Pop Stars

Name your pup after your favourite pop singer or musician.

Female

Adele
Alanis
Alicia
Ariana
Beyonce
Britney
Chaka
Cher
Dionne
Diva
Dixie
Enya
Franklin
Gaga
Jessie
Kiki
LeAnn
Lennox
Macy
Madonna
Miley
Missy
Rihanna
Shakira
Shania
Tammy
Tori
Whitney

Male

Bieber
Bowie
Clapton
Dean
Denver
Elton
Elvis
Hammer
Hendrix
Huey
Jackson
Jagger
Jimi
Jovi
Lennon
Moby
Ozzy
Prince
Ringo
Tupac
Wonder
Zappa

Bob's Book of Dog Names

Colours

Inspired by
 White

Alaska
Almond
Angel
Angelica
Arctic
Aspen
Astrid
Bianca
Blanc
Blizzard
Casper
Chalky
Clay
Coconut
Cotton
Cottonball
Cottontail
Crystal
Elsa
Eskimo

Frosty
Ice
Iceman
Icicle
Ivory
Jon Snow
Lace
Latte
Milky
Moon
Moonlight
Pearl
Polar
Quartz
Seashell
Shell
Snow
Snow White
Snowball
Snowdrop
Snowflake
Snowstorm
Snowy
Star
Starlight
Sugar
Talc
Twinkle
Vanilla
Winter

Inspired by

🐾 Black

Ace
Bean
Bear
Berry
Blackjack
Brownie
Caviar
Cinder
Cocoa
Coffee
Coke
Cola
Cole
Darth
Dice
Diesel
Domino
Dusk
Ebony
Flint
Goth
Guinness
Ink
Inky
Jade
Java
Jet

Liquorice
Magic
Nero
Midnight
Night
Noir
Onyx
Oreo
Panther
Pepper
Pepsi
Puma
Raven
Rolo
Sable
Shade
Shadow
Soot
Starling
Tar
Thunder
Vader
Velvet

Snuppy was the world's first cloned dog, created using a cell from the ear of an Afghan Hound in Seoul, Korea, in 2005. He lived for a decade and bred successfully.

Inspired by

🐾 Brown

Acorn
Auburn
Autumn
Bronze
Brownie
Brun
Bruno
Cappuccino
Caramel
Cedar
Chester
Chestnut
Choco
Chocolate
Cider
Cinnamon
Cocoa
Coffee
Cookie
Copper
Espresso
Fawn
Fern
Forrest
Fudge
Hazel
Hazelnut

Hide
Jasper
Leather
Maple
Mink
Mocha
Nutmeg
Rusty
Sepia
Teak
Tetley
Timber
Toffee
Whisky
Woody

Inspired by

🐾 Yellow/Gold

Bee/Bea
Bumble
Buttercup
Butterscotch
Crackers
Custard
Dandy
Dijon
Flax
Goldie
Honey

Jasmine
Lemon
Milkshake
Mustard
Old Yeller
Old Yellow
Peanut
Pecan
Popcorn
Primrose
Saffron
Sahara
Sandy
Sun
Sunny
Sunshine
Syrup
Waffle
Yeller

Inspired by
Red

Amber
Bambi
Berry
Blaze
Big Red
Bordeaux
Brandy
Burgundy
Cabernet
Cherry
Chilli
Clifford
Coral
Cranberry
Crimson
Damson
Ember
Ferrari
Flame
Firecracker
Foxy
Fuego
Ginger
Jam
Ladybug
Lava
Malbec
Marmalade
Mateus
Merlot
Monarch
Old Red
Paprika
Pinot
Pumpkin
Redwood
Robin

Rose
Rhubarb
Rory
Rosso
Rouge
Ruby
Russet
Rusty
Salsa
Scarlett
Shiraz
Sunrise
Sunset

Inspired by

Grey/Blue/Silver

Agate
Argent
Ash
Azure
Bailey
Birch
Blade
Bullet
Cobalt
Dove
Earl Grey
Fog

Foggy
Ghost
Glimmer
Glitter
Granite
Lady Grey
Misty
Moonstone
Ocean
Pebble
Pewter
Phantom
Sapphire
Silver
Silver Shadow
Shady
Sharky
Slate
Smoky
Smudge
Speckles
Spirit
Steel
Sterling
Stone
Teal
Tinder
Tinsel
Whisper
Wisp

Themes

Inspired by

 Movies

Canine characters in famous films. Disney dogs are listed separately.

Algonquin – Poodle in *Elvira, Mistress of the Dark*

Ambrosius – Old English Sheepdog in *Labyrinth*

Argus – Irish Red and White Setter in *Familiar Strangers*

Babydoll – German Shepherd in *Heavy Petting*

Backup – Pit Bull in *Veronica Mars*

Baxter – Border Terrier in *Anchorman: The Legend of Ron Burgundy*

Beethoven – St Bernard in *Beethoven*

Benji – Mixed breed in *Benji*

Boi – Yorkshire Terrier in *High School Musical II*

Bruiser – Chihuahua in *Legally Blonde*

Buddy – Golden Retriever in *Air Bud*, and Bloodhound in *Cats & Dogs*

Butch – Kangal Shepherd in *Cats & Dogs*

Cherokee – Golden Retriever in *Scream 3*

Chico – Australian Cattle Dog in *Secret Window*

Chinook – Alaskan Malamute in *Trail of the Yukon*

Chum – Labrador Retriever in *Spanglish*

Clue – Basset Hound in *The Adventures of Mary-Kate and Ashley*

Colossus – Bulldog in *Van Wilder*

Cujo – St Bernard in *Cujo*

Daisy – Beagle in *John Wicks*, Golden Retriever in *Grand Torino*, and Staffordshire Bull Terrier in *Snatch*

Daphne – Poodle in *Look Who's Talking Now*

Devon – Border Collie in *A Dog Year*

Diggs – German Shepherd in *Cats & Dogs and The Revenge of Kitty Galore*

Django – Pug in *Django Unchained*

Dog – Australian Cattle Dog in *Mad Max 2: The Road Warrior*

Dolores – Pomeranian in *Double Take*

Dottie – Maltese in *Coming to America*

Bob's Book of Dog Names

Eddie – Labrador Retriever in *The Fabulous Baker Boys*

Edison – Old English Sheepdog in *Chitty Chitty Bang Bang*

Edward – Cardigan Welsh Corgi in *The Accidental Tourist*

Einstein – Bearded Collie in *Back to the Future* trilogy

Elway – Basset Hound in *The Smurfs*

Engels – Maltese in *Hail, Caesar!*

Ernie – Brussels Griffon in *Sweet November*

Fang – Mixed breed in *Vampire Dog*

Flealick – Jack Russell Terrier in *Babe 2: Pig in the City*

Fly – Border Collie in *Babe*

Frank – Pug in *Men in Black*

Friday – Jack Russell Terrier in *Hotel for Dogs*

Gladstone – Bulldog in *Sherlock Holmes*

Gus – Siberian Husky in *Iron Will*

Hachi – Akita Inu in *Hachi: A Dog's Tale*

Hank – Great Dane in *The Truth about Cats & Dogs*

Harvey – Golden Retriever in *ET: The Extra Terrestrial*

Hercules – English Mastiff in *The Sandlot*

Hintza – Rhodesian Ridgeback in *A Far Off Place*

Hobo – German Shepherd in *The Littlest Hobo*

Hooch – French Mastiff in *Turner & Hooch*

Hubble – Border Terrier in *Good Boy*

Jack – Jack Russell Terrier in *The Artist*

Jackyl – Chihuahua in *Dude, Where's My Car?*

Jasper – Cocker Spaniel in *Rebecca*

Jerry Lee – German Shepherd in *K9*

Jessie – Border Collie in *Animal Farm*

Kavik – German Shepherd in *The Courage of Kavik the Wolf Dog*

Lassie – Rough Collie in *Lassie Come Home*

Lenny – Mixed breed in *Lenny the Wonder Dog*

Lester – German Shepherd in *Halloween*

Lloyd – Pug in *Norbit*

Lou – Beagle in *Cats & Dogs*

Lucky – Mixed breed in *Dr Dolittle*

Maggie – Labrador Retriever in *The Wild River*

Marley – Labrador Retriever in *Marley and Me*

Matisse – Border Collie in *Down and Out in Beverly Hills*

Max – Mixed breed in *How the Grinch Stole Christmas*

Milo - Jack Russell Terrier in *The Mask*

Missy – St Bernard in *Beethoven's 2nd*

Moses – Chihuahua in *Meet the Fockers*

Mr Beefy – Bulldog in *Little Nicky*

Nanook – Alaskan Malamute in *The Lost Boys*

Ned – Bulldog in *The Number 23*

Nerak – Scottish Terrier in *The Watcher in the Woods*

Nevins – Terrier mix in *The Cat in the Hat*

Old Yeller – Black Mouth Cur in *Old Yeller*

Otis – Jack Russell Terrier in *Son of the Mask*

PB – Bull Terrier in *Babe 2: Pig in the City*

Peek – Chinese Crested in *Cats & Dogs*

Plugger – Mixed breed in *A Million Ways to Die in the West*

Poppy – Chihuahua in *Mars Attacks!*

Porthos – Great Pyrenees in *Finding Neverland*

Puffy – Border Terrier in *There's Something About Mary*

Rainy – German Shepherd in *Cool Dog*

Rambo – Bulldog in *Mannequin*

Reno – Briard in *Top Dog*

Rin Tin Tin – German Shepherd in *The Adventures of Rin Tin Tin*

Rocks – Mixed breed in *Look Who's Talking Now*

Sadie – Border Collie in *The Conjuring*

Sam – Old English Sheepdog in *Cats & Dogs*

Samantha – German Shepherd in *I am Legend*

Sandy – Airedale Terrier in *Annie*

Saxon – German Shepherd in *Hot Fuzz*

Skeletor – Greyhound in *50/50*

Skip – Jack Russell Terrier in *My Dog Skip*

Skipper – Welsh Corgi in *Robinson Crusoe*

Snots – Rottweiler in *National Lampoon's Christmas Vacation*

Sonny – French Bulldog in *Due Date*

Sparky – Jack Russell Terrier in *Michael*

Spike – Rottweiler in *Alien 3*

Thor – German Shepherd in *Bad Moon*

Toto – Cairn Terrier in The *Wizard of Oz*

Uggie – Parsons Russell Terrier in *The Artist*

Verdel – Brussels Griffon in *As Good as it gets*

Winn-Dixie – Berger Picard in *Because of Winn-Dixie*

Zero – Ghost dog in *The Night Before Christmas*

Zowie – Mixed breed in *Pet Sematary Two*

Inspired by

 **Disney Dogs**

Character names of animated and live action dogs in Disney movies and cartoons

Alpha – Doberman Pinscher in *Up*

Andrew – Bearded Collie in *Mary Poppins*

Angus – Bulldog in *Mr Magoo*

Angel – Shiba Inu in *Lady and the Tramp II*

Annette – Cocker Spaniel in *Lady and the Tramp* and *Lady and the Tramp II*

Beta – Rottweiler in *Up*

Blackie – Puppy in *101 Dalmatians*

Blob – Puppy in *101 Dalmatians*

Blot – Puppy in *101 Dalmatians*

Bolivar – St Bernard pet of Donald Duck

Bolt – German Shepherd in *Bolt*

Boris – Borzoi in *Lady and the Tramp*

Bowser – Puppy bought by Goofy

Bravo – Puppy in *101 Dalmatians*

Bruno – Bloodhound in *Cinderella*

Buck – Alaskan Malamute in *Eight Below*

Bugley – Puppy in *101 Dalmatians*

Buster – Rottweiler/Doberman Pinscher cross in *Lady and the Tramp II* and Dachshund in *Toy Story*

Butch – Bulldog, Pluto's nemesis

Cadpig – Puppy in *101 Dalmatians*

Cash – Spanish Hound in *The Fox and the Hound 2*

Chance – Bulldog in *Homeward Bound: The Incredible Journey*

Chief – Irish Wolfhound in *The Fox and the Hound*

Chiffon – Old English Sheepdog in *The Shaggy Dog*

Chloe – Chihuahua in *Beverly Hills Chihuahua*

Collette – Cocker Spaniel in *Lady and the Tramp* and *Lady and the Tramp II*

Copper – Bloodhound in *The Fox and the Hound*

Corky – Puppy in *101 Dalmatians*

Delgado – German Shepherd in *Beverly Hills Chihuahua*

Danielle – Cocker Spaniel in *Lady and the Tramp* and *Lady and the Tramp II*

DeSoto – Doberman Pinscher in *Oliver & Company*

Dewey – Siberian Husky in *Eight Below*

Dinah – Dachshund, Pluto's girlfriend

Dipper – Puppy in *101 Dalmatians*

Dipstick – Puppy in *101 Dalmatians*

Dixie – Saluki in *The Fox and the Hound*

Dodger – Terrier mix in *Oliver & Company*

Dot – Puppy in *101 Dalmatians*

Dude – Mixed breed in *Descendants*

Dug – Golder Retriever in *Up*

Einstein – Great Dane in *Oliver & Company*

Fidget – Puppy in *101 Dalmatians*

Fifi – Pekingese, Pluto's girlfriend

Flapper – Puppy in *101 Dalmatians*

Francis – Bulldog in *Oliver & Company*

Francois – Boston Terrier in *Lady and the Tramp II*

Freckles – Puppy in *101 Dalmatians*

Frou-Frou – Yorkshire Terrier in *Beauty and the Beast*

Georgette – Poodle in *Oliver & Company*

Gamma – Bulldog in *Up*

Goofy – Hound in *A Goofy Movie*

Jewel – Puppy in *101 Dalmatians*

Jock – Scottish Terrier in *Lady and the Tramp*

Jolly – Puppy in *101 Dalmatians*

Lady – Cocker Spaniel in *Lady and the Tramp* and *Lady and the Tramp II*

Lafayette - Basset Hound in *The Aristocats*

Latch – Puppy in *101 Dalmatians*

Lenny – Puppy in *101 Dalmatians*

Lucky – Puppy in *101 Dalmatians*

Max – Siberian Husky in *Eight Below*

Max Goof – Goofy's son in *A Goofy Movie*

Maya – Siberian Husky in *Eight Below*

Mooch – Old English Sheepdog in *Lady and the Tramp II*

Nana - St Bernard in *Peter Pan*

Nosey – Puppy in *101 Dalmatians*

Old Jack – Siberian Husky in *Eight Below*

Otis – Chinese Crested in *Lady and the Tramp II*

Papi – Chihuahua in *Beverly Hills Chihuahua*

Patch – Puppy in *101 Dalmatians*

Peg – Pekingese in *Lady and the Tramp*

Penny – Puppy in *101 Dalmatians*

Pepper – Puppy in *101 Dalmatians*

Percy – Pug in *Pocahontas*

Perdita – Mum in *101 Dalmatians*

Persephone – Poodle in *Frankenweenie*

Pip – Beagle in *Spooky Buddies*

Pluto – Mixed breed, *Mickey Mouse*

Pokey – Puppy in *101 Dalmatians*

Pongo – Dad in *101 Dalmatians*

Puddles – Puppy in *101 Dalmatians*

Purdy – Puppy in *101 Dalmatians*

Quark – Jack Russell in *Honey, I Shrunk the Kids*

Reggie – Bullmastiff/Bulldog cross in *Lady and the Tramp II*

Rolly – Puppy in *101 Dalmatians*

Rita – Saluki in *Oliver & Company*

Roscoe – Doberman Pinscher in *Oliver & Company*

Rowdy – Mixed breed in *Summer of the Monkeys*

Roxanne – Love interest for Max in *A Goofy Movie*

Ruby – Afghan Hound in *Lady and the Tramp II*

Salter – Puppy in *101 Dalmatians*

Scamp – Mixed breed in *Lady and the Tramp II*

Scratchy – Scottish Deerhound in *Lady and the Tramp II*

Scud – Bull Terrier in *Toy Story*

Shadow – Golden Retriever in *Homeward Bound: The Incredible Journey*, and Alaskan Malamute in *Eight Below*

Shorty – Siberian Husky in *Eight Below*

Sleepy – Puppy in *101 Dalmatians*

Slinky – Dachshund in *Toy Story*

Smokey – Puppy in *101 Dalmatians*

Spanky – Puppy in *101 Dalmatians*

Spark – Puppy in *101 Dalmatians*

Sparky – Irish Wolfhound in *Lady and the Tramp II* and Bull Terrier in *Frankenweenie*

Speedy – Puppy in *101 Dalmatians*

Sport – Puppy in *101 Dalmatians*

Spotty – Puppy in *101 Dalmatians*

Stella – Bloodhound in *The Princess and the Frog*

Sultan – Yorkshire Terrier in *Beauty and the Beast*

Swift – Puppy in *101 Dalmatians*

Talbot – Great Dane in *The Sword in the Stone*

Thunder – Puppy in *101 Dalmatians*

Tiger – Great Dane in *The Sword in the Stone*, and puppy in *101 Dalmatians*

Tito – Chihuahua in *Oliver & Company*

Toby – Basset Hound in *The Great Mouse Detective*

Toughy – Mixed breed in *Lady and the Tramp*

Tramp – Schnauzer mix in *Lady and the Tramp*

Truman – Siberian Husky in *Eight Below*

Trusty – Bloodhound in *Lady and the Tramp*

Two-Tone – Puppy in *101 Dalmatians*

Wags – Puppy in *101 Dalmatians*

Whitie – Puppy in *101 Dalmatians*

Wizzer – Puppy in *101 Dalmatians*

Yoyo – Puppy in *101 Dalmatians*

Inspired by

 Cartoon Dogs

Character names of cartoon canines that don't come from the Disney kennels.

Ace (the Bat Hound) – German Shepherd, *Batman*, DC Comics

Aramis – Springer Spaniel, *Dogtanian and the Three Muskehounds*

Athos – St Bernard, *Dogtanian and the Three Muskehounds*

Astro – Great Dane, *The Jetsons*, Hanna-Barbera

Bandit – English Bulldog, *Jonny Quest*, Hanna-Barbera

Brian (Griffin) – Golden Retriever mix, speaking sidekick of Stewie in *Family Guy*, Fox Broadcasting Company

Bob's Book of Dog Names

Clifford – The Big Red Dog, books by Norman Bridwell followed by a TV series and film

Deputy Dawg – Mixed breed Florida deputy sheriff, created by Terrytoons

Dogmatix – White Terrier companion of Obelix in the French comic book series *Asterix*

Dogtanian – Mixed breed, *Dogtanian and the Three Muskehounds*

Droopy – Basset Hound from MGM Cartoons

Foo-Foo – Poodle, Walter the Softy's dog in *The Beano* comic, DC Thomson

Fred Basset – Basset Hound star of long-running *Daily Mail* comic strip by Alex Graham

Griswald – Bulldog who makes occasional appearances in *Top Cat*, Hanna-Barbera

Gnasher - Abyssinian wire-haired tripehound, Dennis the Menace's pet in *The Beano*, DC Thomson

Gnatasha - Abyssinian wire-haired tripehound/Poodle cross, Gnasher's daughter who appeared in *The Beezer*, *The Topper* and *The Beano* comics, DC Thomson

Gnipper - Abyssinian wire-haired tripehound/Poodle cross, Gnasher's son in *The Beano*, DC Thomson

Gromit – Beagle, *Wallace & Gromit*, Aardmann Animations

Bob's Book of Dog Names

Hector – Bulldog, appeared in various *Looney Tunes* and *Merrie Melodies* cartoons, Warner Bros

Hotdog – Old English Sheepdog mix, Archie Comics

Huckleberry Hound – Blue hound, Hanna-Barbera

Jake – Bulldog, *Adventure Time*, Cartoon Network

Jesse – Herbert's withered old dog in *Family Guy*, Fox Broadcasting Company

Krypto – Labrador, Superman's pet dog makes regular appearances in comic books from DC Comics and has featured in numerous TV shows and films

Marmaduke – Great Dane, star of long-running newspaper comic strip by Brad Anderson then live action movie released in 2010

Mr Peabody – Beagle, first appeared in *The Adventures of Rocky and Bullwinkle*, Jay Ward, and later revived in *The Mr Peabody & Sherman Show*, for Netflix

Mutley – Mixed breed, Dick Dastardly's sidekick with the rasping chuckle in *Wacky Races* and *The Perils of Penelope Pitstop*, Hanna-Barbera

Odie – Dachshund/Beagle mix, drooling sidekick of *Garfield*, created by Jim Davis

Porthos – German Shepherd, *Dogtanian and the Three Muskehounds*

Santa's Little Helper – Greyhound, family pet in *The Simpsons*, Fox Broadcasting Company

Scooby-Doo – Great Dane and sidekick of Shaggy in the long running Hanna-Barbera cartoon series *Scooby-Doo, Where Are You!* and subsequent films

Scrappy-Doo – Great Dane puppy, nephew of Scooby-Doo

Snoopy – Beagle, first appeared in Charles M Schulz's long-running *Peanuts* comic strip, alongside Charlie Brown and friends, in 1950, and, alongside his wee birdie pal Woodstock, far out-grosses the kids in terms of popularity and merchandising

Snowy – Fox Terrier, Tin Tin's dog in Belgian cartoonist Herge's *The Adventure of Tin Tin*

Spot – Cocker Spaniel, *Spot the Dog* by Eric Hill

Spunky – Miniature Bull Terrier, Rocko's dog in Nickelodeon cartoon series *Rocko's Modern Life* and comic books

Created by artist George Studdy, **Bonzo** was the world's first cartoon dog, appearing in the London-based *Sketch* magazine in 1922. The chubby white pup's popularity quickly soared, both in the UK and around the world, and in 1924 he starred in his first animated feature, entitled *Sausage Snatching Sensation*.

Inspired by Soap Stars

Audrey – The Kennedy's Cairn Terrier appeared in Australian soap *Neighbours* for a decade until her death in 2011.

Bossy – The Australian Kelpie replaced Audrey in *Neighbours* in 2012.

Bouncer – Golden Labrador appeared on *Neighbours* for six years, from his debut as a puppy on February 4, 1987. During that time he lived at three addresses, survived road accidents, fathered puppies, got lost, was poisoned by mushrooms, and saved Madge from a chip pan fire.

Eccles – Border Terrier and Barlow family pet in *Coronation Street*, inherited from Blanche Hunt.

Monica – Adopted by *Coronation Street*'s Tyrone in 1999 and named after Courtney Cox's character in *Friends*, the greyhound appeared in the ITV soap until 2008.

Ozzy – Hairdresser Maria's Black Labrador in *Coronation Street*.

Peanut – Dachshund belonging to Kirk and Beth Sutherland in *Coronation Street*.

Roly – The character was originally cast as a German Shepherd but the Poodle got the part, sharing *EastEnders*' Queen Vic with Den, Angie and Sharon Watts from the outset, retiring in 1993.

Rover – *Coronation Street's* Steve McDonald's Jack Russell/Corgi cross was played by actor Simon Gregson's own pet, **Cookie**.

Schmeichel – Dumped on Tyrone's doorstep, the Great Dane passed to young Chesney in *Coronation Street* and the pair quickly became an inseparable double-act.

Wellard – First appearing in 1994, the Belgian Tervuren Shepherd was *EastEnders*' longest serving pet. Loyal companion of Robbie Jackson and latterly Gus Smith, the character was killed off in 2008. Male on screen, Wellard was played by three bitches, **Zenna**, her daughter **Chancer**, and granddaughter **Kyte**.

Willy – A constant source of innuendo, Ethel's pug Willy was named after her late husband and accompanied her wherever she went in *EastEnders*' Albert Square.

The world's first canine movie star was collie **Rover** (real name **Blair**) who appeared in the short British film *Rescued by Rover* (the story of a dog who leads his master to a kidnapped baby) in 1905. It proved an instant hit with audiences.

Bob's Book of Dog Names

Inspired by

🐾 Blue Peter

The world's longest running children's TV show, the BBC's *Blue Peter* is well known for its pets. Since it was first broadcast in 1958, 10 dogs have appeared alongside the human hosts

Petra – Mixed breed Petra was the first *Blue Peter* dog, appearing between 1962 and 1977, initially with Christopher Trace and Valerie Singleton. However, she is best known as sidekick to Peter Purves. After her death, she was immortalised in bronze, the sculpture standing in front of London's Television Centre before being moved to the Blue Peter garden in 1984. In 2011, it moved again, to studios in Salford, Manchester.

Patch – One of Petra's puppies, Patch joined new presenter John Noakes in 1965.

Shep – The excitable Border Collie is one of the most famous Blue Peter dogs. Bought in 1971 to replace Patch, who died in May of that year, he was the long-time partner of Noakes and became the top dog in 1977 when Petra passed away.

Goldie – The Golden Retriever named by viewers joined the show in 1978 as a puppy, together with owner and presenter Simon Groom. When she gave birth to a litter of pups, all but one was given to the Guide Dogs for the Blind Association.

Bonnie – Goldie's remaining pup, took over from her mum in 1986 and has the distinction of being the only one of the show's pets to receive a Blue Peter badge.

Mabel – Border Collie and the first rescue dog to join the show, in 1996, she had the distinction of having one blue and one brown eye. She appeared for over 14 years, retiring on March 30, 2010.

Lucy – Another long-serving pet, the Golden Retriever appeared on screen for 12 years, leaving viewers devastated when she died from a cancer in April 2011.

Meg - Border Collie and trained sheepdog, she belonged to presenter and County Durham farmer Matt Baker and appeared on the show until 2006.

Barney – Irish Setter/Dachshund cross, the former stray was adopted by presenter Helen Skelton, joining the team in 2009 and retiring in 2013.

Henry – Beagle/Basset Hound, rescued by the Dogs Trust, he was the 10th dog to join Blue Peter, first appearing in May 2019.

🐾 🐾 🐾 🐾 🐾

Mary, Queen of Scots, was accompanied to her execution on February 8, 1587, by her loyal Skye Terrier **Geddon** who cowered under her skirts as her head was chopped off.

Bob's Book of Dog Names

Inspired by

🐾 Sitcoms and Series

Buck – The Bundy family's Briard in *Married with Children*

Buster – Beagle in *The Wonder Years*

Chamsky – Bulldog in *Everybody Loves Raymond*

Cinnamon – Raj's Yorkshire Terrier in *The Big Bang Theory*

Claude – Poodle in *The Beverly Hillbillies*

Colin – Miniature Schnauzer in UK sitcom *Spaced*

Diefenbaker – Wolf/dog cross in Canadian Mountie comedy drama *Due South*

Dog – Columbo's imaginatively named Basset Hound in the eponymous US detective series

Duke – Bloodhound in *The Beverly Hillbillies*

There are between 380 and 400 breeds of dog in the world, according to the Federation Cynologique Internationale (FCI), which holds the official register. The number fluctuates as new breeds are recognised and others deleted.

Eddie – Jack Russell Terrier (real name **Moose**) who reportedly earned £10,000 an episode appearing alongside Martin Crane in *Frasier*

Flash – Basset Hound and long-eared canine companion of Sheriff Rosco Purvis Coltrane in *Dukes of Hazzard*

Freeway – Lowchen in US detective series *Hart to Hart*

Jack – Sheepdog mix in *Little House on the Prairie*

K9 – *Doctor Who's* robot dog

Lucky – American Cocker Spaniel replacement for **Buck** in *Married with Children*

Maximillian – Bionic German Shepherd in *The Bionic Woman*

Queequeg – Scully's Pomeranian in *The X-Files*

Roger – Mixed breed family pet in BBC comedy drama *The Durrells*

Rowlf the Dog – Scruffy brown dog on *The Muppet Show*

Spunky – The Fonz's Terrier mix in *Happy Days*

Sweetie – Adopted mutt in *Diary of a Wimpy Kid: Dog Days* by Jeff Kinney

Wilson – Jim's unruly Belgian Tervuren Shepherd (and only friend) in *Friday Night Dinner*. The character was killed off in the final episode of series five and replaced by Great Dane/Poodle cross **Milson** in series six

Inspired by Literature

Canine characters in some well-known books.

Bobby – Skye Terrier who sat by his master's grave in *Greyfriar's Bobby*, by Eleanor Atkinson

Bull's-eye - Bill Sikes' dog in *Oliver Twist*, by Charles Dickens

Bumpy – Noddy's dog in the books by Enid Blyton

Fang – Hagrid's Mastiff in the *Harry Potter* series, by J K Rowling, and one of Farmer Maggot's dogs in *The Lord of the Rings*

Garrick – Demelza's dog in *Poldark*, by Winston Graham

Grip – One of Farmer Maggot's dogs in J R R Tolkein's *The Lord of the Rings*

Jip – Dora Spenlow's Spaniel in *David Copperfield*, by Charles Dickens

Josef – St Bernard in *Heidi*, by Johanna Spyri

Kep – Collie in *The Tale of Jemima Puddle-Duck* by Beatrix Potter

Laska – Hunting dog in Leo Tolstoy's *Anna Karenina*

Montmorency – Fox Terrier in *Three Men in a Boat* by Jerome K Jerome

Nana – Newfoundland nanny of the Darling children in *Peter Pan* by J M Barrie

Pilot – Mr Rochester's Newfoundland in *Jane Eyre*, by Charlotte Bronte

Ripper – Marjorie Dursley's dog in *Harry Potter and the Prisoner of Azkaban*, by J K Rowling

Scamper – Janet's dog in *The Secret Seven*, by Enid Blyton

Timmy – George's faithful brown mongrel in *The Famous Five*, by Enid Blyton

Wolfp – One of Farmer Maggot's dogs in J R R Tolkein's *The Lord of the Rings*

Inspired by Video Games

From *Animal Crossing* to *Grand Theft Auto*, dogs have taken their pixilated place in the world of video games.

Alice – *The Last of Us Part II*

Angelo – *Final Fantasy Part VIII*

Barbas – *The Elder Scrolls V: Skyrim*

Barkspawn – *Dragon Age: Origins*

Bill Grey – *Star Fox 64*

Boney – *Mother 3*

Boomer – *Far Cry 5*

Brown – *Rule of Rose*

Cheese Legs – *Lisa: The Painful*

Chop – *Grand Theft Auto V*

Diamond Dog – *Metal Gear Solid V: The Phantom Pain*

Digby – *Animal Crossing*

Dinky Di – *Mad Max*

Doggo – *Undertale*

Dogmeat – *Fallout* (series)

Floyd – *Jumpstart 1st Grade*

Frankie – *Jumpstart* (series)

Gizmo – *Jumpstart Adventures 4th Grade: Sapphire Falls*

Growlithe – *Pokemon*

Harriet – *Animal Crossing*

Hewie – *Haunting Ground*

Inceptor – *Final Fantasy VI*

Isabelle – *Animal Crossing*

Meeko – *The Elder Scrolls V: Skyrim*

Riley – *Call of Duty: Ghosts*

Roach – *The Witcher 3: Wild Hunt*

Ros – *Assassin's Creed Odyssey: The Fate of Atlantis Part 1*

Rush – *Mega Man 3*

Shadow – *Dead to Rights*

Sif – *Dark Souls*

Whiskey – *Commandos 2: Men of Courage*

Inspired by

Harry Potter

Some dog friendly names from the Harry Potter books and films.

Barty

Bellatrix

Black

Bones

Broom

Diggory

Draco

Dumbledore

Dursley

Fang

Fire

Fudge

Gaunt

Goyle

Hagrid

Harry

Howler

Hufflepuff

Lily

Ludo

Luna

Lupin

Magic

Malfoy

Marvolo

Minerva

Molly

Muggle

Phineas

Phoenix

Price

Quid

Quill

Raven

Remus

Riddle

Ron

Rowena

Scabbers

Sirius

Snape

Tonks

Voldemort

Wanda

Weasley

Henry VIII's second wife, Anne Boleyn, had two dogs, a hunting greyhound, **Urian**, and a small lapdog, possibly Havanese, called **Pourquoi**, who died tragically after falling out of a window. In Tudor times small dogs were fed bread to keep them docile.

Inspired by

Outlander

The canine cast of historical drama *Outlander*.

Bouton – Poodle/Dachshund cross

Bozo – Newfoundland

Bran – Staghound

Elphin

Jehu – Terrier

Jocky

Herbet

Ludo – King Charles Cavalier Spaniel

Luke – Terrier

Mars

Nairn – Staghound

Rollo – Irish Wolfhound/wolf cross

Smoky – Newfoundland

Inspired by

Game of Thrones

If you are a fan, this popular historical drama offers some dramatic ideas for names, whether human or direwolf.

Aemon

Alton

Amory
Areo
Arryn
Arya
Balon
Bolton
Bran
Brienne
Bronn
Davos
Ellaria
Gilly
Grenn
Greyjoy
Hallyne
Hodor
Hound
Jamie
Jaqen
Leaf
Locke
Lyanna
Myranda
Ned
Olyvar
Orell
Osha
Pypar
Rast
Raven

Robb
Roose
Ros
Sandor
Sansa
Shae
Snow
Stark
Talisa
Tarly
Theon
Thorne
Tormund
Tyrion
Varys
Waif
Yoren

Direwolves

Grey Wind
Ghost
Lady
Nymeria
Summer
Shaggydog

Singer Barbra Streisand cloned pet dog **Samantha**, producing replica puppies **Violet** and **Scarlett**.

Bob's Book of Dog Names

Inspired by The Gods

The Greek and Roman gods are a rich source of inspiration for a mighty moniker.

Aether (Greek) – God of light

Ananke (Greek) – Goddess of inevitability, compulsion and necessity

Aphrodite (Greek) – Goddess of beauty, love, desire and pleasure

Apollo (Roman/Greek) – God of music, healing and truth, and twin of **Diana**

Ares (Greek) – God of courage, war, bloodshed and violence

Argos – Faithful canine companion of Odysseus

Artemis (Greek) – Virgin goddess of the hunt, wilderness, animals and the Moon

Asteria (Greek) – Goddess of nocturnal oracles and falling stars

Athena (Greek) – Goddess of reason, wisdom, intelligence, skill, peace, warfare, battle strategy and handicrafts

Atlas (Greek) – God forced to carry the heavens upon his shoulders by Zeus

Aurora (Roman) – Goddess of dawn

Bacchus (Roman) – God of wine, civilization and law

Bellona (Roman) – Goddess of war.

Cerberus (Roman) – The three-headed dog that guarded the underworld

Ceres (Roman) – Goddess of agriculture, harvest, and the seasons

Chaos (Greek) – Initially genderless but later described as the female personification of nothingness from which all existence sprang

Chronos (Greek) – God of time

Cupid (Roman) – Son of **Venus**, he carried a bow and arrow and shot people to make them fall in love

Diana (Roman) – Goddess of hunting and animals, twin of **Apollo**

Demeter (Greek) – Goddess of grain, agriculture, harvest, growth and nourishment

Eos (Greek) – Goddess of the dawn

Erebus (Greek) – God of darkness and shadow

Eros (Greek) – God of love

Faunus (Roman) – God of the forest, fields, and plains

Flora (Roman) – Goddess of flowers and of the season of spring

Fortuna (Roman) – Goddess of luck

Hemera (Greek) – Goddess of day

Hera (Greek) – Queen of the gods and goddess of marriage, women, childbirth, heirs, kings and empires

Hercules (Roman) – Son of **Jupiter** with a mortal mother, he was half god, half human

Hermes (Greek) – God of boundaries, travel, trade, communication, language, writing, cunning and thieves

Hestia (Greek) – Virgin goddess of the hearth, home, domesticity and chastity

Juno (Roman) – Wife of **Jupiter** and goddess of women and fertility

Jupiter (Roman) – King and god of thunder and lightning

Leto (Greek) – Goddess of motherhood

Mars (Roman) – Son of **Jupiter** and **Juno** and god of war

Mercury (Roman) – God of travellers and tradesmen, messenger of the gods

Minerva (Roman) – Goddess of wisdom, learning, arts and industry

Nemesis (Greek) – Goddess of retribution

Neptune (Roman) – Brother of **Jupiter** and god of the sea

Nyx (Greek) – Goddess of the night

Orpheus (Roman) – Son of **Apollo** and **Calliope**, the most famous musician in the ancient world

Pan (Greek) – God of shepherds and flocks

Pandora (Greek) – The first mortal woman, fashioned from clay by the gods

Pegasus (Roman) – A winged horse

Perses (Greek) – God of destruction

Pluto (Roman) – Brother of **Jupiter**; god of the underworld

Poseidon (Greek) – God of the sea, rivers, floods, droughts and earthquakes

Prometheus (Greek) – God of fire and creator of mankind

Rhea (Greek) – Goddess of fertility, motherhood and the wild mountains

Selene (Greek) – Goddess of the Moon

Terra (Roman) – Goddess of the Earth

Venus (Roman) – Goddess of love and beauty

Veritas (Roman) – Goddess of truth

Vesta (Roman) – Sister of **Jupiter** and goddess of hearth and home

Vulcan (Roman) – God of blacksmiths and volcanoes

Zeus (Greek) – King of the gods, ruler of Mount Olympus, and god of the sky, weather, thunder, lightning, law, order and justice

Inspired by Stars and Constellations

If the Gods do not answer your prayers, perhaps it is worth looking to the heavens.

Alasia (star)

Altair (star)

Aquila (constellation)

Ara (constellation)

Aries (constellation)

Avoir (star)

Bellatrix (star)

Capella (star)

Carina (constellation)

Castor (star)

Chara (star)

Crux (constellation)

Draco (constellation)

Electra (star)

Elnath (star)

Gemini (constellation)

Hadar (star)

Icarus (star)

Leo (constellation)

Lynx (constellation)

Lyra (constellation)

Mintaka (star)

Mira (star)

Miram (star)

Mizar (star)

Morava (star)

Nashira (star)

Nunki (star)

Orion (constellation)

Pegasus (constellation)

Perseus (constellation)

Polaris (star)

Puppis (constellation)

Phoenix (constellation)

Ran (star)

Sabik (star)

Scorpius (constellation)

Sirius (star)

Shaula (star)

Spica (star)

Taurus (constellation)

Laika may be the most famous Russian space dog but, in the 1950s and 60s, the Soviet Union launched dozens of canines into the sky as part of its space program. Most survived and some were sent on multiple missions. **Dezik** and **Tsygan** made the first sub-orbital flight in 1951 while **Veterok** and **Ugolyok** hold the record for the longest space flight by dogs, spending 21 days in orbit in 1966.

Inspired by

🐾 Royal Dogs

Queen Elizabeth II is well known for her love of Corgis, a passion shared by her parents, King George VI and Queen Elizabeth the Queen Mother.

However, the Royal love affair with canine companions dates back much further, to King Charles I who popularised the King Charles Spaniel in the 17th century. Queen Victoria and her husband Prince Albert were the first to document their collection of domestic dogs.

Victoria, who often sketched the dogs in the Royal Kennels, established at Windsor in the early 1840s, kept Dachshunds, Collies, Pugs and Pomeranians while her successor, King Edward VII, had a love of Terriers and his son King George V maintained this tradition, adding working dogs like Labradors.

King George VI bought the first Pembroke Welsh Corgi in 1933 – **Dookie** – and since taking the throne in 1952, the Queen has owned over 30, all descended from **Susan**, gifted to her on her 18th birthday.

She later bred Dorgis, crossing her Corgi **Tiny** with her sister Princess Margaret's Dachshund **Pipkin**.

Prince Charles has favoured Jack Russell Terriers, some of their names taken from characters in AA Milne's *Winnie the Pooh*, while sister Anne's canines of choice are English Bull Terriers, one of which infamously mauled the Queen's Corgi **Pharos**, resulting in his death.

🐾 The Queen

Corgis

Bee

Brush

Bushy

Carol

Crackers

Dookie

Emma

Foxy

Heather

Holly

Honey

Jane

Linnet

Muick

Monty

Noble

Pharos

Ranger

Sherry

Smoky

Sugar

Tiny

Whisky

Bob's Book of Dog Names

Whisper

Willow

Dorgis

Berry

Brandy

Candy

Chipper

Cider

Fergus

Harris

Pickles

Piper

Tinker

Vulcan

Cocker Spaniels

Bisto

Flash

Oxo

Span

Spick

🐾 Prince Charles

Jack Russell Terriers

Beth

Bluebell

Pooh

Roo

Tigga

🐾 Princess Anne

Bull Terriers

Dotty

Florence

🐾 William and Kate

Lupo – Black English Cocker Spaniel adopted by Prince William, Duke of Cambridge and Catherine, Duchess of Cambridge, in 2012

🐾 Harry and Meghan

Guy – Beagle

Pula – Black Labrador

🐾 Princess Beatrice and Princess Eugenie

Norfolk Terriers

Cici

Ginger

Jack

Orange

Teddy

🐾 Princess Margaret

Choo-Choo – Tibetan Lion, childhood pet of Princess Elizabeth and Princess Margaret

Johnny – Dachshund

Pipkin – Dachshund

Rawley – Cavalier King Charles Spaniel

King Edward VII

Alex – Borzois owned by Queen Alexandra

Caesar – Norfolk Terrier, loyal to the end, he followed the funeral procession of his master and is immortalised in stone sitting at the feet of the King's tomb in St George's Chapel, Windsor

Vassilka – Borzoi, a gift to King Edward VII and Queen Alexandra from Tsar Alexander III and Tsarina Maria Feodorovna

Queen Victoria

Cairnach – Skye Terrier

Dandie – Skye Terrier

Dash – Companion of the Queen during her adolescence and early years of her reign

Eos – Greyhound, accompanied Prince Albert from Germany to England

Hector – Deerhound

Islay – Skye Terrier

Marco – Pomeranian named after explorer Marco Polo

Noble – Collie

Sharp – Collie

Swan – White greyhound

Turi – Pomeranian who stayed by Queen Victoria's side on the day she passed away

---

French Queen Marie Antoinette arrived from Austria with her beloved pet Pug **Mops** and was gifted a dog she nicknamed **Mignon**.

Inspired by

Heroic Dogs

These are the dogs that have put their lives on the line during both conflict and peacetime, including recipients of the Dickin Medal, an award for gallantry instituted in 1943 by Maria Dickin, founder of the People's Dispensary for Sick Animals (PDSA), to honour the work of animals during the Second World War. Recipients include not only dogs but also pigeons, horses and a cat.

Apollo – The NYPD German Shepherd and his handler were the first search and rescue dog team to arrive on scene following the collapse of the World Trade Center towers on September 11, 2001. Apollo received the Dicken Medal on behalf of all search and rescue dogs who assisted in the aftermath of the terrorist attacks

Balto – In 1925, the Siberian Husky led a daring sled run through blizzards to ferry a life-saving serum to the people of Nome in Alaska, saving them from a deadly outbreak of Diphtheria

Bamse – Mascot of the Royal Norwegian Navy minesweeper *Thorodd*, which spent much of the Second World War based in Montrose, Scotland, the St Bernard knocked a knifeman into the sea and later saved a crew member from drowning. It is said he also rounded up drunken sailors from the pubs of Montrose at the end of shore leave. Posthumously awarded the PDSA Gold Medal in 2006.

Barry – Between 1800 and 1812 the St Bernard saved the lives of over 40 people in the mountains around the St Bernard Pass, Switzerland

Belka and **Strelka** – Less well known than **Laika**, Russia's first dog in space, these two mixed breeds were the first animals to survive an orbital flight, circling Earth aboard *Sputnik 5* on August 19, 1960

Bob – The mixed breed served with the 6th Battalion Queen's Own Royal West Kent Regiment and was the first dog to be presented with the Dickin Medal.

Cairo – The Belgian Shepherd was deployed with US Navy SEALs in *Operation Neptune Spear* in which terrorist leader Osama bin Laden was killed in 2011

Cappy – A Doberman Pinscher credited with saving the lives of 250 US Marines during the Battle of Guam in 1944 by alerting them to approaching Japanese soldiers

Chips – The US Army sentry dog, a German Shepherd/Collie/Husky mix, is believed to be the most decorated of all Second World War service dogs

Conan – Deployed to Syria with US Delta Force commandos in 2019, the Belgian Shepherd chased down a wanted ISIS leader who was subsequently captured and killed. Conan sustained minor injuries in the operation but recovered fully

Donnchadh – Scottish king Robert the Bruce's faithful bloodhound

Jack – Known locally as Swansea Jack, the flat-coated Black Retriever was awarded for his life-saving work. Born in 1930, he rescued at least 25 people from the waters of Swansea docks and the River Tawe

Judy – The only dog to be officially registered as a prisoner of war during the Second World War, Pointer Judy was awarded the Dickin Medal in 1946 for helping to keep morale high among fellow inmates of the Japanese stockade

Laika – As the sole occupant of *Sputnik 2*, the mongrel from Russia was the first dog to orbit Earth, paving the way for human space travel. Sadly she did not make it home alive

Mancs – The Hungarian rescue dog was known for his keen

sense of smell and the clear signal he sent rescuers to indicate survivors under the rubble of earthquakes

Midnight – Saved from the devastation of Hurricane Katrina, which swept through New Orleans in 2005, the Black Lab joined the rescue effort following Hurricane Sandy, seven years later

Moustache – Serving with the French Grenadier during the French Revolutionary Wars and Napoleonic Wars, the legendary French Poodle is said to have lost an ear at the Battle of Marengo and captured an Austrian spy, recovered the regiment's standard and lost a leg in an artillery blast at the Battle of Austerlitz

Nemo – Blinded in one eye by gunshot during a Vietnam War battle in 1966, the US Air Force German Shepherd fought on, hurling himself at enemy soldiers before crawling on top of his injured handler to protect him from further harm

Peritas – Legend has it that the dog saved Alexander the Great from an attack by Persian King Darius III

Rip – A Second World War hero, the mixed breed sniffed out scores of survivors buried in the rubble of London's streets during the air raids of the Blitz. Awarded the Dickin Medal in 1945

Rob – The Collie served with Britain's elite Special Air Service (SAS) during the Second World War and is said to have made over 20 parachute drops during the North African Campaign. Awarded the Dickin Medal in 1945

Sheila – The Collie helped rescue four American airmen after their plane crashed in the Cheviot Hills, on the Anglo-Scottish border, during a blizzard in December 1944. She was the first civilian animal awarded the Dickin Medal

Smoky – Found by an American soldier, the abandoned Yorkshire Terrier's small size and intelligence was perfect for communications work in the South Pacific during the Second World War. In addition to helping string wires between outposts, she warned soldiers of incoming fire

Stubby – A stray Boston Bull Terrier adopted by American soldiers, during the First World War, 'Sergeant' Stubby warned men of mustard gas attacks and located wounded soldiers in the trenches of north France

---

One of the most decorated canine war veterans, **Sinbad** served aboard the US Coast Guard cutter *George W Campbell* for 11 years and saw combat during the Second World War.

Bob's Book of Dog Names

Trakr – The German Shepherd detection dog found the last survivor of the September 11, 2001, terrorist attacks in the rubble of the World Trade Center, New York

Inspired by

Working Dogs

Names inspired by notable military, police, rescue, guide and other working dogs.

Agata

Ana

Antis

Baillie

Bart

Beauty

Bilbo

Bing

Bunko

Chesty

Chinook

Dakota

Don

Endal

Flo

Frida

Gabi

Gandalf

Gander

Irma

Kira

Kuga

Kuno

Lex

Lucca

Nico

Orca

Oscar

Owney

Philly

Polo

Rags

Roselle

Salty

Sarbi

Sasha

Sinbad

Sombra

Sully

Susie

Theo

Thorn

Tich

Togo

Treo

Trixie

Wanda

Zanjeer

Inspired by

🐾 Nobility

Noble names with a regal ring.

Alexander
Alexandra
Alexis
Alfred
Anastasia
Augustus
Baron
Caesar
Camilla
Catherine
Charles
Charlotte
Cleo
Contessa
Countess
Czar
Diana
Duchess
Duke
Earl
Edward
George
Hamlet
Henry
Ivan
Josephine

Kaiser
Khan
King
Knight
Lady
Laird
Lord
Magnus
Majesty
Monarch
Napoleon
Noble
Pharaoh
Prince
Princess
Queen
Queenie
Raja
Rex
Rian
Sceptre
Sheba
Spartan
Squire
Sultan
Victoria
Viscount
Winston

Bob's Book of Dog Names

Inspired by

World Leaders

Names bestowed on pet dogs by presidents and prime ministers.

Barney – One of former US President George W Bush's two Scottish Terriers

Blondi – German Shepherd gifted to fascist dictator Adolf Hitler by his deputy Martin Bormann in 1941. Remained by his side until the end

Bo – One of two Portuguese Water Dogs owned by former US President Barack Obama

Buddy – Former US President Bill Clinton's Chocolate Labrador

Buffy – Bulgarian Shepherd owned by Russian President Vladimir Putin

Champ – One of two German Shepherds belonging to US President Joe Biden and his wife Jill

Checkers – Former US President Richard Nixon's Cocker Spaniel

Dilyn – Something of a rarity in 10 Downing Street where cats have ruled the roost, the white Jack Russell cross lives with Prime Minister Boris Johnson and wife Carrie Symonds

Fala – Former US President Franklin D Roosevelt's Scottish Terrier

Fido – Yellow mixed breed owned by former US President Abraham Lincoln

Him and **Her** – Pair of Beagles that belonged to former US President Lyndon Johnson

Konni – Female black Labrador owned by Russian President Vladimir Putin

Lennu – Boston Terrier pet of Finnish President Sauli Niinistö

Liberty – Former US President Gerald R Ford's Golden Retriever

Major – Second of two German Shepherds belonging to US President Joe Biden and his wife Jill

Mrs Beazley – The second of former US President George W Bush's two Scottish Terriers

Nemo – Black Labrador cross rescued by French president Emmanuel Macron and his Brigitte

Paddy – Former British Prime Minister Harold Wilson's yellow Labrador

Pete – Former US President Theodore Roosevelt's Bull Terrier, rumoured to have bitten so many people he was exiled from the White House

Pushinka – A gift from Russia, former US President John F Kennedy's mixed breed was one of six puppies delivered by space dog Strelka. Pushinka went on to have four puppies, fathered by Kennedy's dog **Charlie** and these were jokingly referred to as 'pupniks'

Rex – Former US President Ronald Reagan's pet dog

Rufus – During the Second World War, British Prime Minister Winston Churchill was frequently accompanied by his chocolate-brown Miniature Poodle Rufus. Churchill was devasted when Rufus was run over and killed in 1947, but was persuaded to adopt another, rather sickly Poodle, naming him **Ruffus II**. Also had a Bulldog called **Dodo**

Spot Fetcher – Former US President George W Bush's English Springer Spaniel, named after Texas Rangers baseball player Scott Fletcher

Sunny – The second of two Portuguese Water Dog owned by former US President Barack Obama

Yume – Russian President Vladimir Putin's Akita

Inspired by

Explorers

Pioneering names for pups that love to explore.

Aldrin

Armstrong

Bruce

Cabot

Columbus

Cook

Drake

Fiennes

Hanno

Hillary

Hudson

Livingstone

Magellan

Mallory

Marco

Parry

Polo

Raleigh

Scott

Shackleton

Stafford

Stanley

Tenzing

Inspired by

Scientists

Discover some genius names from the world of science.

Ampere

Archimedes

Aristotle

Bunsen

Cousteau

Curie

Darwin

Einstein

Faraday

Bob's Book of Dog Names

Fleming
Galen
Galileo
Hippocrates
Hubble
Maxwell
Moseley
Nightingale
Nobel
Pythagoras
Volta
Watt

Inspired by

Great Outdoors

Names from around the British Isles, ideal for active dogs that love being out of doors.

Abb
Abbey
Affric
Ailsa
Airlie
Allt
Alva
Alvie
Amble
Angus
Anster
Appin

Arkle
Arran
Atholl
Avoch
Avon
Ayr
Ben
Beinn
Birnam
Blair
Blyth
Boulmer
Braan
Brae
Brecon
Brora
Bruar
Buckie
Buddo
Bute
Cairn
Cairnie
Calder
Camber
Cambo
Canna
Cannich
Canvey
Chester
Clach

Clifton	Flint
Clova	Filby
Clunie	Filey
Clyde	Findon
Connel	Fraser
Corbie	Garry
Corran	Glen
Corrie	Handa
Cowie	Harris
Cromer	Humber
Cuillin	Inch
Cullen	Insh
Cyrus	Inver
Dee	Isla
Denny	Joppa
Derry	Jura
Devon	Liath
Dollar	Lenzie
Don	Kirby
Dover	Kirk
Dune	Kishorn
Eccles	Kyle
Eden	Larch
Elie	Largo
Ellen	Leven
Ellon	Lewis
Eriska	Lorn
Ethie	Lossie
Feshie	Lunan
Fleet	Lundin

Bob's Book of Dog Names

Luss	Ralia
Lynton	Rannoch
Lyon	Reay
Macduff	Rhue
Mallie	Rhum
Markie	Roker
Meikle	Rona
Morar	Ross
Moray	Rubha
Morven	Sandwood
Moy	Shiel
Muckle	Shin
Muick	Shuna
Nairn	Skerry
Naver	Skye
Ness	Sleat
Nessie	Snook
Nevis	Spey
Newton	Storr
Ordie	Strathy
Penrose	Tain
Preston	Talla
Raasay	Tarf
	Tay
	Tigh
	Torr
	Torran
	Torrin
	Tweed
	Windsor

> King Henry VIII kept Spaniels, Beagles and Greyhounds but his favourites were lapdogs **Cut** and **Ball** who wore velvet collars embossed with gold and silver Tudor roses.

Inspired by

🐾 Trees and Flora

Let nature inspire you.

Alder

Apple

Aspen

Beech

Birch

Blackthorn

Bluebell

Bracken

Bramble

Broom

Buttercup

Cedar

Chestnut

Daisy

Elm

Fern

Flora

Heather

Hazel

Holly

Iris

Ivy

Juniper

Larch

Lily

Meadow

Oak

Pansy

Pine

Plum

Primrose

Rose

Rowan

Rye

Sitka

Spruce

Thorn

Violet

Walnut

Willow

Inspired by

🐾 Seas and Oceans

Immerse yourself in these deep and meaningful monikers.

Adriatic

Arctic

Baffin

Baltic

Banda

Bay

Beaufort

Bering

Biscay

Caspian

Coral

Java

Kara

Scotia

Solomon

Sulu

Tasman

Inspired by

Technology

Search out a techie name for your cyber surfing canine.

Adobe

Alexa

Android

Apache

Atari

Beta

Binary

Bing

Bit

Bot

Byte

Bug

Cache

Chip

Clara

Clarus

Cloud

Codec

Cookie

Core

Cortana

Cyber

Data

Dell

Digit

Etsy

Giga

Gizmo

Google

Hacker

Hashtag

Insta

Java

Kernal

Kindle

Linux

Mac

Matrix

Mega

Meme

Micro

Nano

Pentium

Pixel

Pro

Quora

Sega

Bob's Book of Dog Names

Siri
Sonic
Spam
Tiff
Tinder
Tosh
Vector
Widget
Wifi
Wiki
Zip

Inspired by

Cars

Four-wheeled motoring icons that drive a bond with our four-legged friends.

Alfa
Alpine
Aston
Astra
Austin
Bentley
Bond
Bugatti
Buick
Camaro
Capri
Carrera
Cavalier
Chevvy
Clio
Cobra
Colt
Cooper
Corsa
Cougar
Diablo
Diesel
Dino
Dodge
Elise
Evo
Ferrari
Healey
Herbie
Hummer
Imp
Jag
Jensen
Juke
Laguna
Lexus
Lusso
Martin
Miura
Mercedes
Midget
Mini
Minx

Bob's Book of Dog Names

Mondeo
Morgan
Morris
Noble
Nova
Phantom
Pinto
Porsche
Princess
Puma
Ranger
Rapier
Riley
Rio
Riva
Robin
Romeo
Rover
Royce
Shadow
Shelby
Sierra
Sunbeam
Tamora
Tasmin
Taurus
Tesla
Trabie
Triumph
Turbo

Tuscan
Twingo
Viva
Zonda

Inspired by

Perfect Pairs

For a pair of pups, consider these well-known double acts.

Abbott and Costello
Adam and Eve
Adam and Joe
Anna and Elsa
Ant and Dec
Anthony and Cleopatra
Apples and Pears
Asterix and Obelix
Aunt and Uncle
Bacon and Eggs
Bangers and Mash
Barbie and Ken
Barnaby and Jones
Barnum and Bailey

The highest jumping dog in the world is **Feather** who leapt 191.7cm (75.5 inches) in Maryland, USA, on September 14, 2017.

Basil and Sybil
Batman and Robin
Beavis and Butthead
Benson and Hedges
Bert and Ernie
Beauty and the Beast
Beer and Nuts
Ben and Jerry
Bill and Ben
Bill and Ted
Black and Decker
Black and White
Bobby and Pam
Bodie and Doyle
Bonnie and Clyde
Bread and Butter
Brian and Stewie
Brother and Sister
Bubble and Squeak
Bullwinkle and Rocky
Bugs Bunny and Daffy Duck
Burton and Taylor
Butch Cassidy and the Sundance Kid
Cagney and Lacey
Cain and Abel
Calvin and Hobbes
Cannon and Ball
Caramel and Sea Salt
Chandler and Monica
Charles and Di

Chas and Dave
Cheese and Crackers
Cheese and Onion
Chips and Cheese
Chocolate and Mint
Clark and Lois
Coffee and Doughnuts
Cream and Sugar
Crick and Watson
Crockett and Tubbs
Dalziel and Pascoe
Dastardly and Mutley
David and Goliath
Dawn and Dusk
Day and Night
Dempsey and Makepeace
Den and Angie
Dennis and Gnasher
Dick and Dom
Dick and Jane
Dolce and Gabanna
Donald and Daisy
Dumb and Dumber
Ebony and Ivory
Edina and Patsy
Fire and Brimstone
Fish and Chips
Flora and Fauna
Fox and the Hound
Frasier and Niles

Bob's Book of Dog Names

Fred and Wilma
French and Saunders
Fry and Laurie
Gavin and Stacey
George and Mildred
Gin and Tonic
Hale and Pace
Hall and Oates
Ham and Cheese
Ham and Mustard
Hamburger and Fries
Hanna and Barbera
Hansel and Gretel
Hans Solo and Chewbacca
Hawkeye and BJ
Him and Her
Holmes and Watson
Homer and Marge
Ice and Lemon
Ike and Tina
Itchy and Scratchy
Jack and Jill
Jack and Vera
Jake and Amy
Jeeves and Wooster
Jekyll and Hyde
Jesus and Mary
Kermit and Miss Piggy
King and Queen
Kirk and Spock

Krystal and Blake
Kylie and Jason
Lady and the Tramp
Lady Mary and Matthew
Laurel and Hardy
Laverne and Shirley
Lennon and McCartney
Liam and Noel
Little and Large
Liver and Onion
Lone Ranger and Tonto
Mac and Cheese
Mario and Luigi
Marks and Spencer
Marlin and Dory
Mary and Joseph
Mash and Gravy
Mickey and Minnie
Milk and Cookies
Mister and Missus
Mitchell and Webb
Morecambe and Wise
Mork and Mindy
Morse and Lewis
Mulder and Scully
Mum and Dad
Napoleon and Josephine
Naughty or Nice
Oatmeal and Raisins
Once or Twice

Orpheus and Eurydice
Pancakes and Maple Syrup
Peaches and Cream
Peanut Butter and Jelly
Peas and Carrots
Pen and Paper
Penn and Teller
Phineas and Ferb
Pinky and Perky
Pinky and The Brain
Pooh and Piglet
Popeye and Olive Oyl
Porgy and Bess
Posh and Becks
Punch and Judy
Reeves and Mortimer
Ren and Stimpy
Richard and Judy
Rick and Morty
Ricky and Bianca
Robin and Maid Marion
Rock and Roll
Rod and Emu
Rodger and Hammerstein
Roger and Jessica
Romeo and Juliet
Romulus and Remus
Rosencrantz and Guildenstern
Rosie and Jim
Rhubarb and Custard

Ross and Rachel
Rum and Coke
Sage and Onion
Salt and Pepper
Salt and Vinegar
Samson and Delilah
Scooby-Doo and Shaggy
Scott and Charlene
Simon and Garfunkel
Smokey and the Bandit
Smith and Wesson
Snoopy and Woodstock
Song and Dance
Sonny and Cher
Sooty and Sweep
Spaghetti and Meatballs
Spick and Span
Stanley and Livingstone
Starsky and Hutch
Steak and Kidney
Strawberries and Cream
Sugar and Spice
Sweet and Savoury
Tarzan and Jane
Tease and Seas
Terry and June
Thelma and Louise
Thunder and Lightening
Tom and Barbera
Tom and Jerry

Bob's Book of Dog Names

Tomato and Basil
Torvill and Dean
Tweedle Dee and Tweedle Dum
Tweetie and Sylvester
Victor and Margaret
Victoria and Albert
Wallace and Gromit
Wayne and Garth
Whisky and Soda
Wile E Coyote and Road Runner
Will and Grace
William and Kate
Willow and Tara
Woody and Buzz Lightyear
Yin and Yang
Zig and Zag

Clarkson, Hammond and May
Cowley, Boddie and Doyle
Faith, Hope and Charity
Father, Son and the Holy Spirit
Harry, Ron and Hermoine
Huie, Diewy and Louie
Jimmy, Henry and Tommy
Larry, Curly, and Moe
Lock, Stock and Barrel
Luke, Leia and Han Solo
Mickey, Donald and Goofy
Miley, Lilly and Oliver
Nachos, Cheese and Salsa
Snap, Crackle and Pop
Spock, McCoy, Kirk
Tom, Dick and Harry

Inspired by

Terrific Trios

If three is the magic number, these famous trios might just come up trumps.

Alvin, Theodore, and Simon
Aragorn, Legolas and Gimli
Aramis, Athos and Porthos
Bacon, Lettuce and Tomato
Brody, Hooper and Quint
Buffy, Willow and Xander
Burger, Fries, Coke
Charlotte, Emily and Anne

Bob's Book of Dog Names

A-Z

The A-Z contains all the names already listed in the book, plus hundreds more in alphabetical order

A

Abb
Abbey
Abe
Acacia
Ace
Acorn
Ada
Adam
Adi
Adonis
Adriatic
Aduke
Aero
Aeron
Aether
Affric
Agata
Agate
Aida
Ailsa
Ainsley
Airlie
AJ
Ajax
Ajay
Akira
Alan
Alana

Alanis
Alasia
Alaska
Alba
Albie
Alder
Aldrin
Aled
Alesha
Alessa
Alex
Alexander
Alexandra
Alexis
Alfa
Alfie
Alfred
Algonquin
Ali
Alina
Alisha
Alissa
Allegra
Allt
Ally
Alma
Almond
Alpha
Alpina
Alpine

Altair	Anwen
Alva	Anya
Alvie	Aphrodite
Alvin	Apollo
Ama	Appin
Amber	Apple
Amble	April
Ambrosius	Aquila
Americano	Ara
Amira	Aramis
Amos	Aran
Ampere	Arbuckle
Amy	Archer
Ana	Archie
Ananke	Archimedes
Anastasia	Arctic
Andie	Ares
Andrew	Argent
Angel	Argon
Angus	Argos
Anise	Argus
Anna	Aria
Annette	Ariana
Annie	Ariel
Annika	Aries
Anster	Arin
Ant	Aristotle
Antis	Arkle
Anton	Armstrong
Antonio	Arnie

Bob's Book of Dog Names

Arran	Augusta
Arrow	Augustus
Art	Aurora
Artemis	Austen
Arty	Austin
Arvin	Autumn
Arwen	Ava
Asa	Avery
Ash	Avia
Asha	Aviva
Asher	Avoch
Ashwin	Avoir
Asia	Avon
Aslan	Axa
Aspen	Axel
Assam	Ayla
Asteria	Ayr
Aston	Azra
Astoria	Azure
Astra	
Astrid	
Astro	# B
Asya	
Athena	Babe
Athole	Babs
Atholl	Baby
Athos	Babydoll
Atlas	Bacchus
Atticus	Backup
Auburn	Bacon

Baffin	Baxter
Bailey	Baylee
Baillie	Baylor
Ball	Bea
Balti	Bean
Baltic	Beast
Balto	Beau
Bambi	Beaufort
Bamse	Beauty
Banda	Bebe
Bandit	Beach
Bang	Beaker
Banger	Beavis
Banjo	Becca
Banshee	Becks
Barbas	Becky
Barista	Bee
Barker	Beer
Barkspawn	Beethoven
Barley	Belka
Barnaby	Bella
Barney	Bellatrix
Baron	Belle
Barrel	Bellona
Barry	Ben
Bart	Benji
Basha	Benny
Basil	Benson
Batman	Bentley

Bob's Book of Dog Names

Bering	Biscuit
Berkley	Bitty
Berry	Blackberry
Bert	Blackbird
Bertha	Blackheart
Bertie	Blackie
Bess	Black Jack
Bessie	Blackthorn
Beta	Blade
Beth	Blair
Betsy	Blaise
Betty	Blake
Beyonce	Blanc
Bianca	Blanche
Bibi	Blaze
Bieber	Bliss
Big Red	Blizzard
Biggles	Blob
Bilbo	Blondie
Bill	Blood
Billie	Blossom
Billy	Blot
Bing	Blue
Bingo	Bluebell
Birch	Blueberry
Birdie	Bluebird
Birnam	Bluejay
Biscay	Blyth
Biscotti	Bo

Bob
Boba
Bobby
Bobo
Bodger
Bodie
Bojo
Bolivar
Bolt
Bond
Bones
Boney
Bonnie
Bonzo
Boots
Bordeaux
Boris
Boss
Bossy
Boulmer
Bouncer
Bounty
Bourbon
Bowie
Bowser
Bozo
Braan
Bracken
Brad

Brady
Brae
Bramble
Bran
Brandy
Brax
Brecon
Bree
Breeze
Brennan
Brett
Brew
Bria
Brian
Bridie
Brimstone
Brioche
Britney
Britt
Brock
Brody
Brogan
Bronte
Bronze
Brooke
Broom
Brora
Brown
Brownie

Bob's Book of Dog Names

Bruar	Bumpy
Bruce	Bunko
Bruiser	Bunsen
Brun	Burger
Bruno	Burgundy
Brush	Burrito
Brutus	Bush
Bryn	Bushy
Bubba	Buster
Bubblegum	Butch
Bubbles	Butter
Buck	Butterball
Buckie	Buttercup
Buckley	Butterfly
Bud	Butternut
Buddo	Butterscotch
Buddy	Buttons
Buena	Buzz
Buffy	Byron
Bugatti	
Bugley	
Buick	

C

Bulla
Buller
Bullet
Bulls-eye
Bullwinkle
Bulstrode
Bumble

Cabernet
Cabot
Cacey
Cadpig
Caesar
Cafall

Cagney
Cain
Caira
Cairn
Cairnach
Cairnie
Cairo
Cajun
Cal
Calder
Caleb
Calista
Callie
Cally
Calvin
Calypso
Cam
Camaro
Camber
Cambo
Camilla
Candy
Canis
Canna
Cannich
Cannon
Canvey
Capella
Capper
Cappuccino

Cappy
Capri
Cara
Caramel
Carina
Carl
Carlos
Carly
Carmel
Carmen
Carol
Carrera
Carrick
Carrie
Carrow
Carson
Carter
Casey
Cash
Casper
Caspian
Cassius
Castor
Cate
Catherine
Cava
Cavalier
Cavan
Caviar
Cayenne

Bob's Book of Dog Names

Cece	Chaser
Cedar	Chay
Cerberus	Chaz
Ceres	Checkers
Cha Cha	Cheese
Chad	Chelsea
Chai	Chelsey
Chalk	Cher
Chalky	Cherie
Chakka	Cherish
Champ	**Cherokee**
Champagne	Cherry
Chan	Chester
Chance	Chestnut
Chancer	Chesty
Chandler	Chevvy
Chanel	Chewbacca
Chaos	Chewy
Chap	Chico
Chappie	Chief
Chara	Chiffon
Chardonnay	Chilli
Charity	Chinook
Charkie	Chip
Charles	Chipper
Charley	Chips
Charlie	Chippy
Charlotte	Chloe
Chas	Choco
Chase	Chocolate

Choo-Choo	Clouseau
Chop	Clova
Chopper	Clove
Chronos	Clover
Chum	Clue
Churro	Clunie
Chutney	Clyde
Cici	Cobalt
Cider	Cobi
Cinder	Cobra
Cinnamon	Coby
Cindy	Coco
Cisco	Cocoa
CJ	Coconut
Clach	Codi
Clan	Cody
Clapton	Coffee
Clara	Coke
Clark	Cola
Clarkson	Colby
Claude	Cole
Claudia	Collette
Clay	Colin
Cleo	Colm
Cliff	Colossus
Clifford	Colt
Clifton	Comet
Clint	Conan
Clinton	Connah
Clio	Conner

Bob's Book of Dog Names

Connel	Cowley
Connie	Crackers
Conor	Crackle
Conrad	Cranberry
Contessa	Cream
Cook	Crick
Cookie	Crimp
Cooper	Crimson
Copper	Crockett
Cor	Cromer
Cora	Crouch
Coral	Crumble
Coran	Crunchie
Corbie	Crush
Corky	Crusty
Corrie	Crux
Corsa	Crystal
Cortado	Cuba
Cortana	Cubano
Costa	Cube
Costello	Cuillin
Cotton	Cujo
Cottonball	Cullen
Cottonbud	Cupcake
Cottontail	Cupid
Cougar	Curie
Count	Curly
Countess	Cyrus
Cousteau	Czar
Cowie	

D

Dab
Daddy
Daisy
Dakota
Dale
Dali
Dalia
Dalian
Dama
Dame
Damson
Dan
Dana
Dancer
Dandy
Dane
Danger
Dani
Danielle
Danny
Dante
Daphne
Dara
Darby
Darcey
Dario
Darrin
Darth
Darwin
Dash
Dasher
Dave
Dawg
Dawn
Dean
Deano
Deb
Debbie
Dec
Declan
Dee
Deja
Del
Delboy
Delgado
Delia
Della
Delta
Deltic
Demi
Den
Dennis
Denny
Dent
Denver
Deputy Dawg
Dermot
Derry

Bob's Book of Dog Names

DeSoto
Destiny
Dev
Devon
Dewey
Dex
Dexter
Dhal
Di
Diablo
Diamond
Diana
Diane
Dice
Dick
Diddly
Diddy
Diefenbaker
Diego
Diesel
Digby
Diggle
Diggs
Digit
Dijon
Dina
Dinah
Dingo
Dink
Dinky

Dino
Dint
Dionne
Dior
Dipper
Dipstick
Diva
Dixie
DJ
Django
Dobby
Dobs
Doc
Dodge
Dodger
Dodo
Doggo
Dogmatix
Dogtanian
Dolby
Dolcie
Dollar
Dolly
Dolores
Dom
Domino
Don
Donnchadh
Donnie
Donut

Doodle

Dookie

Dora

Dorito

Dot

Dottie

Doug

Doughball

Doughnut

Douglas

Dove

Dover

Draco

Drake

Drax

Dre

Drew

Droopy

Dubois

Duchess

Dude

Duffle

Dug

Duke

Dune

Dusk

Duster

Dustin

Dusty

Dylan

E

Earl

Earl Grey

Ebony

Eccles

Echo

Ed

Eddie

Eden

Edgar

Edie

Edina

Edison

Edward

Eeyore

Effie

Einstein

Elan

Electra

Elf

Eli

Elie

Elise

Ella

Elle

Ellen

Ellie

Elliot

Ellison

Bob's Book of Dog Names

Ellon
Elm
Elnath
Elsa
Elsie
Elton
Elvis
Elway
Ember
Emilio
Emily
Emma
Emmy
Emu
Endal
Engels
Ennis
Enola
Enya
Enzo
Eos
Erebus
Eric
Erica
Erin
Eriska
Eriskay
Ernie
Eros
Errol

Eskimo
Esme
Esmerelda
Espresso
Esra
Essa
Estee
Esther
Ethan
Ethel
Ethie
Etta
Eurydice
Eva
Eve
Evo
Ezme
Ezra

F

Fab
Fabio
Fairy
Faith
Fala
Falco
Falcon
Fang
Fara

Faraday	Fiona
Farina	Fionn
Farley	Fire
Fauna	Firebug
Faunus	Firecracker
Fawn	Firefly
Fay	Firestorm
Feather	Firework
Felson	Fisher
Fen	Fizz
Fergus	Flame
Fern	Flap
Ferrari	Flapjack
Ferris	Flapper
Feshie	Flare
Fidget	Flash
Fido	Flax
Fiennes	Flea
Fiery	Flealick
Fifi	Fleet
Fig	Fleming
Figo	Fletch
Filby	Fletcher
Filey	Fleur
Fin	Flick
Finch	Flicker
Findlay	Flint
Findon	Flip
Fink	Flit
Finn	Flo

Bob's Book of Dog Names

Flock	Fran
Flop	Francis
Floppy	Fracker
Flora	Frackles
Florence	Fraggle
Floss	Francois
Flossy	Franco
Flower	Frank
Floyd	Frankie
Fluff	Franklin
Fluffy	Franz
Fluke	Fraser
Flush	Frasier
Fly	Freckles
Flyer	Fred
Flynn	Fred Basset
Fog	Freddie
Foggy	Fredo
Fonz	Freeway
Fonzie	Frenzy
Foo-Foo	Freya
Ford	Frida
Forrest	Friday
Fortuna	Frito
Fortune	Fritz
Foster	Frodo
Fowler	Frosty
Fox	Frou-Frou
Foxy	Fry
Fozzie	Fryer

Fudge
Fuego
Furbaby
Furry
Fury
Fuzz
Fuzzy
Fynn

G

Gabanna
Gabe
Gabi
Gaby
Gaga
Galen
Galileo
Gambit
Gamble
Gamma
Gandalf
Gander
Garfunkel
Garnet
Garrick
Garry
Garson
Garth
Gator

Gatsby
Gaunt
Gavin
Gecko
Geddon
Geezer
Gem
Gemini
Gemma
Gemstone
Gene
General
Geordie
George
Georgette
Georgia
Georgie
Gerry
Gertie
Ghillie
Ghost
Ghost Rider
Gil
Giles
Gilly
Gimlet
Gimli
Gin
Gina
Ginger

Bob's Book of Dog Names

Gingernut	Granite
Gingersnap	Grant
Gino	Gravy
Giselle	Grayson
Gitana	Greg
Gizmo	Gregor
Gladstone	Gremlin
Glen	Grendel
Glenn	Greta
Glimmer	Gretel
Glitter	Grey
Gnash	Greyjoy
Gnasher	Greystone
Gnatasha	Grey Sea
Gnipper	Grey Wind
Gobber	Grey Wolf
Godiva	Grenn
Godzilla	Gribble
Gold	Griff
Goldie	Griffin
Goldeneye	Grimble
Gollum	Grin
Gonzo	Grip
Goofy	Gripper
Goth	Griswald
Gov	Grizzle
Governor	Grizzly
Goyle	Gromit
Grace	Grouch
Gracie	Growler

Growlithe
Gru
Gruff
Gucci
Guido
Guinness
Gunner
Gus
Gusto
Guy
Gwen
Gyp
Gypsy

H

Hachi
Hadar
Hades
Haggard
Hagrid
Hailey
Hal
Hale
Hall
Halle
Halo
Hamish
Hamlet
Hamm

Hammer
Hammerstein
Hammond
Hammy
Han Solo
Handa
Handy
Hank
Hanna
Hannah
Hanno
Hans
Hansel
Hanson
Happy
Harley
Harmony
Harold
Harper
Harriet
Harris
Harrison
Harry
Hash
Hashtag
Hattie
Haven
Hawkeye
Hazel
Hazelnut

Bob's Book of Dog Names

Heath	Hilton
Heather	Hintza
Heaven	Hippocrates
Hector	Hippy
Heidi	Hoax
Helen	Hobbit
Helena	Hobbs
Hemera	Hobnob
Hemp	Hobo
Hendrix	Hodor
Henley	Hogan
Henna	Holden
Henry	Holly
Hentai	Holmes
Hera	Homer
Herbet	Honey
Herbert	Honor
Herbie	Honour
Hercules	Hooch
Hermes	Hook
Hermione	Hooper
Hero	Hoops
Hestia	Hope
Heston	Hoppy
Hettie	Horatio
Hewie	Hotdog
Hiccup	Houdini
Hicks	Hound
Hide	Howler
Hillary	Huan

Hubble
Huck
Huckleberry
Hudson
Huey
Hufflepuff
Huggy Bear
Hugh
Hugo
Humber
Hummer
Hunt
Hunter
Hurley
Hutch
Huw
Huxley
Hyde

I

Ibby
Icarus
Ice
Icecap
Iceman
Icicle
Icon
Icy
Ida

Ifan
Iggy
Ilsa
Imp
Inca
Inceptor
Inch
India
Indiana
Indie
Indigo
Inferno
Ingot
Ingrid
Inigo
Ink
Inky
Inouk
Insh
Inver
Iola
Iona
Ipsa
Ipsy
Ira
Irca
Iris
Irma
Isa
Isaac

Bob's Book of Dog Names

Isabel	Jacksie
Isabella	Jackson
Isabelle	Jackyl
Isetta	Jacob
Ish	Jade
Isha	Jaffa
Isla	Jag
Islay	Jagger
Isle	Jaguar
Isola	Jaime
Isra	Jak
Itchin	Jake
Itchy	Jam
Itsch	Jammy
Itsy	Jan
Iva	Jana
Ivan	Jane
Ivana	Janey
Ivetta	Jangles
Ivor	Janis
Ivory	Jardine
Ivy	Jarod
Izzy	Jarvis
	Jasmine
J	Jasper
	Java
	Javier
Jace	Jax
Jack	Jay
Jackie	Jazz
Jacko	

JD	Jimi
Jed	Jimmy
Jedi	Jingle
Jeeves	Jinx
Jeff	Jip
Jehu	JJ
Jekyll	Jo
Jelly	Jock
Jen	Jocky
Jenna	Jodi
Jenny	Jodie
Jensen	Joe
Jenson	Joel
Jeremy	John
Jerome	Johnny
Jerry	Jojo
Jersey	Jolie
Jest	Jolly
Jester	Jonah
Jess	Jonas
Jesse	Jones
Jessica	Joppa
Jessie	Jordan
Jet	Jordy
Jethro	Jos
Jetta	Josef
Jewel	Josephine
Jill	Josh
Jim	Joshua
Jimbo	Josie

Jovi
Joy
Jude
Judge
Judy
Juke
Julia
Jules
Julian
Juliet
Julius
July
Jump
Jumper
June
Junior
Juniper
Juno
Jupiter
Jura
Justin

K

K9
Kable
Kacy
Kai
Kaiser
Kale

Kalu
Kane
Kanye
Kara
Karen
Karoo
Kate
Katerina
Katia
Katie
Kato
Katya
Katz
Kavik
Kay
Kayla
Kaycee
Kaylee
Kazak
Kean
Kee
Keefe
Keely
Keir
Kelbie
Kelly
Kelpie
Kelsey
Kelso
Ken

Kendal	Kingsley
Kendra	Kingston
Kendrick	Kink
Kenna	Kintail
Kennedy	Kip
Kenny	Kipper
Kenobi	Kira
Kenzie	Kirby
Kenzo	Kiri
Kep	Kirk
Kermit	Kiro
Kerr	Kirsty
Kerri	Kish
Kerry	Kishi
Kerys	Kishka
Kesia	Kishorn
Kessie	Kismet
Kessler	Kit
Kevin	Kitt
Keya	Kiwi
Khan	Kizzie
Khloe	Knight
Kia	Kobe
Kian	Kody
Kidney	Kona
Kiki	Kong
Kim	Konni
Kimmy	Korma
King	Kray
Kinga	Krill

Bob's Book of Dog Names

Kris
Krissy
Krista
Krypto
Krystal
Kuga
Kuno
Kunzite
Kurt
Kyle
Kylie
Kym
Kyte

L

Lace
Lacey
Lachlan
Lacy
Lad
Laddie
Lady
Ladybird
Ladybug
Lady Grey
Lafayette
Laguna
Laika
Laird

Laker
Lance
Lancer
Lancet
Lancia
Lanta
Lantra
Lara
Larch
Largo
Larry
Laser
Laska
Lass
Lassie
Latch
Latte
Laura
Laurel
Lauren
Laurie
Lava
Laverne
Layla
Lazer
Leaf
Leather
Lee
LeeAnn
Legend

Leia	Lily
Lemon	Limmy
Len	Lin
Lena	Linden
Lennie	Lindor
Lennon	Lindt
Lennu	Linnet
Lenny	Lint
Lenzie	Linus
Leo	Linux
Leon	Linzi
Leroy	Lion
Lester	Lips
Leto	Liquorice
Levi	Little
Lewis	Liver
Lex	Livi
Lexie	Livingstone
Lexus	Liz
Leyla	Lizzie
Liam	Lloyd
Liath	Lobo
Libby	Locke
Liberty	Locket
Lidl	Lok
Lightening	Lola
Lila	Lolita
Lil	Lolly
Lillie	Lolo
Lilly	Lord

Bob's Book of Dog Names

Lori
Lorn
Lorna
Lossie
Lottie
Lotus
Lou
Louie
Louis
Louise
Lowri
Luana
Luc
Lucas
Lucca
Lucia
Lucien
Lucifer
Lucky
Lucy
Ludo
Luigi
Luka
Luke
Lulu
Luna
Lunan
Lundin
Lupin
Lupo

Lurch
Luss
Lusso
Luther
Lyanna
Lyle
Lynn
Lynton
Lynx
Lyon
Lyra

M

Mabel
Mac
Maca
Macallan
Macduff
Mack
McFly
McKinley
McTavish
Macho
Macy
Maddie
Mad Dog
Madge
Madina
Madison

Madonna

Maeby

Mag

Magellan

Maggie

Magic

Magna

Magnus

Maiden

Maisy

Majesty

Major

Makepeace

Malbec

Malc

Malfoy

Mali

Malibu

Mallie

Mallory

Malone

Mancs

Mandy

Manny

Maple

Marco

Margarita

Margot

Maria

Mariah

Mario

Markie

Marley

Marlin

Marlowe

Marmaduke

Marmalade

Mars

Marshall

Martin

Martini

Martha

Marty

Marvolo

Mary

Mash

Matcha

Mateo

Mateus

Matilda

Matisse

Matrix

Matt

Matzoball

Maude

Maui

Maverick

Mavis

Max

Maxi

Bob's Book of Dog Names

Maxim
Maximillian
Maximus
Maxine
Maxwell
May
Maya
Meadow
Meatball
Medea
Meeko
Meg
Mega
Megan
Meikle
Mel
Meme
Mentos
Mercedes
Mercie
Mercury
Mercy
Merle
Merlin
Merlot
Mex
Mica
Mick
Mickey
Micro

Midge
Midget
Midnight
Mignon
Mika
Mike
Mila
Milan
Mildred
Milena
Miley
Milkshake
Milky
Miller
Milly
Milo
Milson
Mimi
Mina
Minch
Mindy
Ming
Minerva
Mini
Mink
Minnie
Mint
Mintaka
Minto
Minty

Minx	Monte
Mira	Montgomery
Miram	Montmorency
Miraz	Monty
Misha	Moo
Mishka	Mooch
Miss	Mookie
Missy	Moon
Mister	Moonlight
Misty	Moonstone
Mitch	Moppet
Mitzi	Mops
Miura	Morar
Mizar	Morava
Mo	Moray
Moby	Morgan
Mocha	Mork
Moe	Morris
Mojito	Morse
Molly	Mort
Momo	Mortimer
Mona	Morven
Monarch	Moseley
Mondeo	Moses
Monet	Moss
Monica	Mouse
Monk	Moustache
Monkey	Moxie
Monroe	Moy
Montana	Muckle

Bob's Book of Dog Names

Muddle	Nano
Muffin	Nanook
Muggle	Napier
Mugsy	Napoleon
Muick	Napper
Mulan	Nappy
Mulder	Napster
Munchkin	Naraka
Muppet	Narco
Murphy	Narita
Murray	Nash
Mustard	Nashira
Mutley	Nashville
Mutt	Nat
Mya	Nate
Myles	Nevaeh
Mylo	Navar
Myranda	Ned
Myron	Nell
Mystic	Nellie
	Nelson
	Nemesis
N	Nemo
	Nena
Nacho	Neneh
Nairn	Neptune
Nala	Nerak
Nana	Nero
Nancy	Ness
Nando	Nessie
Nanny	

Nev
Neve
Nevins
Nevis
Newton
Nibbler
Nibbles
Niblet
Nick
Nickel
Nicky
Nico
Nifty
Niggles
Night
Nightfall
Nighthawk
Nightingale
Nightjar
Nightshade
Nika
Nike
Nikita
Niko
Niles
Ninja
Nipper
Nippet
Nitro
Nirvana

Niven
Noah
Nobby
Nobel
Noble
Noddy
Noel
Noir
Noodle
Norman
Nosey
Nougat
Nova
Nox
Nudge
Nugget
Nunki
Nutella
Nutmeg
Nuts
Nutter
Nutty
Nyla
Nymeria

O

Oak
Oakley
Oates

Bob's Book of Dog Names

Oberon
Obi
Obi-Wan
Ocean
Octavia
Odie
Odin
Oki
Ola
Olaf
Old Red
Old Yeller
Old Yellow
Olga
Olive
Oliver
Ollie
Olly
Olyvar
Omar
Onion
Onyx
Oona
Opal
Ophelia
Oppo
Optimus
Orange
Orbit
Orca

Ordell
Ordie
Oreo
Orion
Orla
Orlando
Orell
Ori
Orpheus
Orville
Osa
Oscar
Osha
Oshie
Osman
Osprey
Ossian
Otis
Otto
Owen
Ox
Oxo
Oz
Ozzy

P

Pablo
Pacey
Paco

Pad	Peg
Paddington	Pegasus
Paddy	Peggy
Pal	Penfold
Palma	Penn
Pam	Penny
Pan	Penny Lane
Pandora	Penrose
Pansy	Pentium
Panther	Pepe
Panto	Peppa
Paprika	Pepper
Paris	Pepsi
Parker	Percy
Parry	Perdita
Pasha	Peridot
Pat	Peritas
Patch	Perky
Patsy	Perry
Paws	Perses
Pavlova	Perseus
Peaches	Pesto
Peaky	Petal
Peanut	Pete
Pearl	Peter
Pebbles	Petra
Pecan	Petula
Peek	Pewter
Peeper	Phantom
Peeps	Pharaoh

Bob's Book of Dog Names

Pharos	Pogo
Philly	Pokey
Phineas	Polar
Phiz	Polaris
Phoebe	Polly
Phoenix	Polo
Picasso	Ponch
Pickles	Pong
Pignoli	Pongo
Pilot	Pooh
Pinch	Pop
Pine	Popcorn
Ping	Popeye
Pink	Popper
Pinky	Poppy
Pinot	Pops
Pinto	Porkchop
Pip	Porky
Piper	Porsche
Pipitty	Porthos
Pippa	Portia
Piri	Poseidon
Pistachio	Possum
Pistol	Prancer
Pixel	Presley
Pixie	Presto
PJ	Preston
Plug	Pretzel
Plum	Price
Pluto	Primo

Primrose
Prince
Princess
Pringles
Pro
Prometheus
Prosecco
Prospero
Puck
Pudding
Puddles
Puddy
Pudge
Pudsey
Puff
Puffball
Puffin
Puffy
Puma
Pumbaa
Pumpkin
Punch
Punk
Punto
Puppis
Purdy
Pushinka
Pushkin
Pypar
Pythagoras

Q

Quark
Quartz
Quasi
Quattro
Quaver
Quayle
Queen
Queenie
Quentin
Quid
Quill
Quince
Quincy
Quinn
Quint
Quintin
Quintus
Quip
Quito
Quixote
Quora

R

Raasay
Rab

Bob's Book of Dog Names

Rabbie	Razzo
Racer	Reay
Rachel	Red
Radar	Redwood
Rafe	Reef
Raff	Reese
Rafferty	Reeves
Raffles	Reggie
Rags	Remus
Rain	Remy
Rainbow	Ren
Raisin	Reno
Raja	Rex
Raleigh	Reya
Ralf	Reza
Ralia	Rhea
Ralph	Rhubarb
Rambo	Rhue
Ramsay	Rhum
Ran	Rian
Randy	Ribbon
Ranger	Ribs
Rannoch	Ribsy
Rapier	Rick
Rascal	Ricky
Raul	Ricochet
Raven	Rider
Rawley	Riddle
Ray	Ridley
Razer	Rihanna

Riley	Roker
Ringo	Rollie
Rin Tin Tin	Rollo
Rio	Rolo
Rip	Roly
Ripley	Roman
Ripper	Roma
Ripple	Rome
Rishi	Romeo
Rita	Romulus
Riva	Ron
River	Rona
Riz	Ronan
Rizla	Roo
Rizzle	Roofus
Rizzo	Rooibos
Roach	Rook
Rob	Rookie
Robb	Roose
Robin	Rory
Robbo	Ros
Robby	Rosa
Robson	Roscoe
Rocco	Rose
Rock	Roselle
Rocket	Rosencrantz
Rocks	Rosie
Rogan	Rosemary
Roger	Ross
Rogue	Rosso

Bob's Book of Dog Names

Rosy

Rouge

Rover

Rowan

Rowena

Rowlf

Roxanne

Roxy

Roy

Royce

Ruaridh

Rubble

Ruben

Rubha

Ruby

Rudy

Rufus

Ruka

Rum

Rumble

Rumi

Rupert

Rush

Russ

Russo

Russell

Russet

Rusty

Ruth

Ryan

Ryder

Rye

S

Sabik

Sable

Sadie

Saffron

Sage

Sahara

Saint

Sake

Sally

Salsa

Salter

Salty

Sam

Samantha

Sambuca

Sammy

Samson

Sancho

Sanday

Sandor

Sandwood

Sandy

Sannah

Sansa

Santa

Sapphire
Sarbi
Sarge
Sasha
Sassy
Saunders
Savannah
Saxon
Scabbers
Scamp
Scamper
Scampi
Scar
Scarlett
Sceptre
Schmeichel
Scooby
Scooby-Doo
Scoot
Scooter
Scorpius
Scotch
Scotia
Scott
Scotty
Scout
Scrapper
Scraps
Scrappy
Scrappy-Doo

Scratchy
Scrumble
Scud
Scully
Seamus
Seashell
Seb
Sega
Selene
Senna
Sepia
Sergio
Seth
Shackleton
Shade
Shadow
Shady
Shae
Shaggy
Shaggydog
Shakira
Shand
Shandy
Shania
Sharky
Sharp
Sharpie
Shasta
Shaula
Shayla

Bob's Book of Dog Names

Sheba	Siri
Sheila	Sirius
Shelby	Sisco
Sheldon	Sitka
Shell	Sixpack
Shep	Skeletor
Sheriff	Skerry
Sherlock	Skip
Sherman	Skipper
Sherry	Skippy
Shiel	Skittles
Shin	Sky
Shiraz	Skye
Shirley	Skyler
Shiva	Slate
Shola	Sleat
Shona	Sleepy
Shooter	Slinky
Shorty	Smithy
Shrimp	Smokey
Shuna	Smudge
Sidi	Snick
Sierra	Snickers
Sif	Sniff
Silver	Sniffer
Silver Shadow	Snook
Simba	Snooky
Simon	Snoop
Sinatra	Snoopy
Sinbad	Snooty

Snots	Spencer
Snow	Spey
Snowball	Spica
Snowdrop	Spice
Snowflake	Spike
Snowstorm	Spinee
Snow White	Spirit
Snowy	Spock
Snuff	Sporty
Snuppy	Spot
Soba	Spotty
Soda	Spruce
Solo	Spunky
Solomon	Squiddly
Sombra	Squidgy
Sonic	Squire
Sonny	Stacey
Soot	Stafford
Sooty	Stag
Sophie	Stamper
Spam	Stan
Spanky	Stanley
Spark	Star
Sparkle	Starbuck
Sparky	Starburst
Sparrow	Stardust
Spartan	Stark
Speckles	Starlet
Spectre	Starlight
Speedy	Starling

Bob's Book of Dog Names

Starsky
Steel
Stella
Sterling
Stew
Stewie
Stomper
Stone
Storm
Stormy
Stormzy
Storr
Strathy
Strauss
Strider
Stryker
Stub
Stubby
Sugar
Suki
Sula
Sully
Sultan
Summer
Summit
Sun
Sunbeam
Sundae
Sundance
Sunday

Sunny
Sunrise
Sunset
Sunshine
Sushi
Susie
Sweetie
Swan
Sweep
Sweetpea
Swift
Sybil
Sydney
Sylvester
Syrup

T

Tabitha
Taffy
Tag
Tain
Taj
Talc
Talisa
Talisker
Talla
Tally
Tam
Tamara

Tammy	Teal
Tamora	Ted
Tan	Teddy
Tango	Tee
Tania	Teebo
Tapas	Teebone
Tar	Teejay
Tara	Tegan
Taran	Teller
Tardy	Tenzing
Tarf	Tequila
Tarik	Tern
Tarka	Terra
Tarly	Terry
Tarn	Tesla
Tarot	Tess
Tarzan	Tessa
Tash	Tetley
Tasker	Tetra
Tasman	Tetris
Tasmin	Tex
Tate	Thai
Tatters	Thelma
Tattoo	Theo
Taurus	Theodore
Tawny	Theon
Tay	Thermo
Taylor	Thimble
Taz	Thog
Teak	Thor

Bob's Book of Dog Names

Thorn	Tizzy
Thorpe	Toast
Thunder	Tobias
Thunderball	Toby
Tia	Tock
Tich	Toffee
Tickles	Toggle
TicTac	Togo
Tiff	Tolkein
Tiffin	Tom
Tiger	Tomatin
Tigger	Tommy
Tigh	Tomtom
Tikka	Tonka
Tilly	Tonks
Tim	Tonto
Timber	Tony
Timmy	Topaz
Tina	Topper
Tinder	Toppy
Ting	Tori
Tinker	Tormund
Tinkerbell	Toran
Tinsel	Tonic
Tintin	Topsy
Tinto	Torr
Tiny	Torrin
Tipper	Tosh
Tipsy	Toto
Tito	Toughy

Toulouse
Trabie
Tracer
Tracker
Trakr
Tramp
Travis
Treacle
Trekr
Trent
Treo
Trev
Trey
Trifle
Trinket
Triumph
Trix
Trixie
Trouble
Troy
Truffle
Truman
Trusty
Tubbs
Tuck
Tucker
Tuco
Tug
Tulip
Tully

Tumnus
Tundra
Tupac
Turbo
Turi
Turner
Tuscan
Tweed
Tweedle
Tweet
Tweetie
Twiggy
Twiglet
Twingo
Twinkle
Twister
Twix
Two-Tone
Tyrion
Tyrone
Tyson

U

Uber
Uggie
Uggs
Uhura
Uli

Bob's Book of Dog Names

Ulla
Ulra
Ulric
Uma
Una
Uno
Urchin
Ursula

V

Vader
Val
Valentine
Valentino
Valka
Valour
Vamp
Van
Vanessa
Vanilla
Vanquish
Vantage
Varys
Vassilka
Vector
Vegas
Velvet
Ventura

Venus
Vera
Verdel
Vesper
Veritas
Vespa
Vesta
Vexy
Vick
Vicky
Victor
Victoria
Vida
Vidal
Vienna
Vigro
Viking
Vimm
Vimto
Vince
Vinci
Vinnie
Viola
Violet
Viper
Virgil
Virginia
Virgo
Visa
Viscount

Vista
Vita
Vito
Viv
Viva
Vixen
Vlad
Vodka
Vogue
Volcano
Voldemort
Volt
Volta
Voltan
Votan
VP
Vulcan

W

Wade
Wafer
Waffle
Waggy
Wags
Waif
Waldo
Waldorf
Walker
Wallace
Walnut

Walt
Walter
Wanda
Wanderer
Wasabi
Watson
Watt
Wayne
Weasley
Webb
Webster
Weechee
Weegee
Wellard
Wellington
Wendy
Wesley
Wesson
Wheezer
Whippy
Whiskey
Whisky
Whisp
Whisper
White Fang
Whitey
Whitney
Whizz
Whizzer
Whoopi

Whoops
Whoopsie
Widdle
Widget
Wifi
Wiggins
Wiki
Wildfire
Wiley
Wilf
Will
William
Willow
Willy
Wilma
Wilson
Windsor
Wink
Winnie
Winona
Winston
Winter
Wise
Wish
Wizard
Wolf
Wombat
Wonder
Woodstock
Woody

Wook
Wookiee
Wooster
Wotsit
Wrecker
Wrigley
Wurzel
Wyatt
Wycliffe
Wyn

X

Xander
Xara
Xena
Xenia
Xherdan
Xhosa
Xhost

Y

Yancy
Yang
Yankee
Yanna
Yap

Yapper
Yappy
Yarrow
Yash
Yasha
Yasmin
Yelper
Yell
Yeller
Yeti
Yin
Yoda
Yogi
Yoko
Yoren
York
Yorkie
Yoyo
Yume
Yumi
Yuri

Z

Zach
Zafira
Zafiro
Zag

Zak
Zane
Zanjeer
Zappa
Zara
Zed
Zed
Zee
Zelda
Zenna
Zephyr
Zero
Zest
Zesty
Zeta
Zeus
Zig
Ziggy
Zinc
Zip
Zippo
Zippy
Zoe
Zoggy
Zoltan
Zonda
Zoot
Zoro
Zulu

Notes

Printed in Great Britain
by Amazon